# SHARING FOOD
*with friends*

# SHARING FOOD
## *with friends*

### CASUAL DINING IDEAS AND INSPIRING RECIPES FOR PLATTERS, BOARDS AND SMALL BITES

**KATHY KORDALIS**

**PHOTOGRAPHY BY MOWIE KAY**

RYLAND PETERS & SMALL
LONDON • NEW YORK

First published in 2017 and reissued in 2021 by Ryland Peters & Small
20–21 Jockey's Fields, London WC1R 4BW
and
341 E 116th St, New York NY 10029
www.rylandpeters.com

10 9 8 7 6 5 4 3 2 1

ISBN: 978-1-78879-382-7

Printed in China

Senior designer Megan Smith
Editors Miriam Catley and Gillian Haslam
Production David Hearn
Art director Leslie Harrington
Editorial director Julia Charles
Publisher Cindy Richards

Food stylist Kathy Kordalis
Food stylist assistant Sarah Fassnidge
Prop stylist Jennifer Kay

Indexer Vanessa Bird

## Notes

• Both British (Metric) and American (Imperial plus US cups) measurements are included here for your convenience, however it is important to work with one set of measurements and not alternate between them within a recipe.

• All spoon measurements are level unless otherwise specified.

• All eggs are medium (UK) or large (US), unless specified as large, in which case US extra-large should be used. Uncooked or partially cooked eggs should not be served to the very old, frail, young children, pregnant women or those with compromised immune systems.

• Whenever butter is used in these recipes, unsalted butter should be used.

• When a recipe calls for the grated zest of citrus fruit, buy unwaxed fruit and wash well before using. If you can only find treated fruit, scrub well in warm soapy water before using.

• When a recipe calls for full-fat cream cheese, it should be white, creamy smooth and have at least 24 per cent fat content, such as Kraft Philadelphia.

• To sterilize preserving jars, wash them in hot, soapy water and rinse in boiling water. Place in a large saucepan and cover with hot water. With the saucepan lid on, bring the water to a boil and continue boiling for 15 minutes. Turn off the heat and leave the jars in the hot water until just before they are filled. Invert the jars onto a clean kitchen cloth to dry. Sterilize lids for 5 minutes by boiling or according to manufacturer's instructions. Jars should be filled and sealed while they are still hot.

• Cheeses started with animal rennet are not suitable for strict vegetarians so read food labelling carefully and, if necessary, check that the cheese you buy is made with a non-animal (microbial) starter. Traditional Parmesan is not vegetarian so we recommend a vegetarian hard cheese (such as Gran Moravia which has the same texture so is ideal for grating) or Parma (a vegan product). There is an increasing number of manufacturers now producing vegetarian versions of traditionally non-vegetarian cheeses, such as Gruyere or Gorgonzola. Check online for suppliers and stockists.

• There are certain health risks associated with whipped cream so always practice food safety by using fresh cream before its expiry date and covering and storing prepared desserts in the refrigerator until ready to serve.

# Contents

# Party planning basics

As far back as I can remember, growing up in Australia my family, however busy they were, always made time to get together. Sometimes, it was casual and sometimes it was more formal. As a Greek Australian, the cultures of Greek feasting and Australian laidback lifestyle have really influenced the way I live, eat and celebrate. Let's face it, Greeks like a party. Marrying into a British family and living in London for the past 13 years have further inspired the ingredients I cook with. London is a place where over 200 cultures meet and live together and they bring with them a cornucopia of recipes, ingredients and customs.

This book is a collection of menus and recipes that, to me, really celebrate fuss-free entertaining. The main purpose of getting together is to spend time together – it's pointless if your guests do not see you. So with a few tips and a general running order, you will be able to entertain effortlessly at home. Some of the menus do require extra preparation and planning but the outcome will be worth it. There are tips on what to buy in and what to make from scratch, how to make the table pretty and how to maximize flavour.

## Getting started

Whether planing a party for a large crowd or having a few friends around, there are a few handy tips you can follow. Most recipes have been written for 4–6 people, but can easily be upped for a larger crowd.

**Know your crowd.** Who are you inviting and what style of food do they like, are there any dietary requirements or vegetarians? Any menu should include a lot of vegetable options, then you have your bases covered.

**Date.** Get the date in the diary. This is not always easy! Living in London where everyone has such busy lives, I find that this is the hardest part of planning a gathering.

**Plan the menu and what you will be drinking.** This is my favourite part. Either follow each table menu fully, mix and match from all the tables or add your own touch. All is perfectly acceptable. It is about sharing time and food with your loved ones and bringing people together.

**Make a shopping list**, which should include simple decorations and/or flowers, all the platters and serving pieces and need not break the bank.

**Plan a cooking schedule.** Work out what can be made ahead and frozen, cooked the day before or on the day, and what you can buy already prepared.

**Make list of equipment needed and potential entertainment.** That need not mean hiring a performer, but pre-selecting music or games that all can share.

**Get help with cleaning after the party**, delegate to loved ones; another sharing moment!

## Feeding a large crowd

No need to get in a flap as you have planned and prepared for this. All the tables in this book have dishes that can be prepared in advance, can sit at room temperature and only a few of the recipe options are served warm. They are all about relaxed entertaining.

**Keep it classic with a few twists.** Choose a selection of dishes that can be made in advance, with easy fresh additions on the day.

## YOUR FREEZER & PANTRY

This list is a good basic list of what you can store in your freezer, fridge and pantry/larder.

**FREEZER**
- Soups
- Pre-made casseroles
- Hummus
- Pizza dough, after its first rise
- Ice – ALWAYS
- Frozen berries
- Smoothie mixes including bananas
- Frozen shrimp
- Good-quality stock
- Flavoured butters
- Broad/fava beans
- Peas

**LARDER/PANTRY**
- Extra virgin olive oil
- Flavourless oils for baking and frying
- Flavoured oils for dressings, such as walnut, sesame, chilli/chile
- Vinegars: balsamic, red-wine, apple cider, sherry
- Spices
- Dried chilli/hot red pepper flakes
- Sea salt, peppercorns
- Soy sauce
- Miso
- Dijon mustard
- Wholegrain mustard

- Capers
- Worcestershire sauce
- Sriracha
- Honey
- Canned beans
- Grains
- Rice
- Passata/tomato paste/sundried tomato paste
- Kalamata olives, green olives
- Artichokes
- All sorts of nuts
- Chocolate
- Green tea
- Wine

**FRIDGE**
- Citrus: oranges, lemons, grapefruit, limes
- Onions
- Leafy greens
- Garlic
- Spring onions/scallions
- Tomatoes
- Fresh herbs
- Parmesan cheese and/or vegetarian option
- Feta cheese
- Greek yogurt
- Eggs

**It is okay to cheat a little.** Buy things in to make it easy for you. A combination of made from scratch and bought items is a nice balance.

**Update the 'buffet'.** With this style of entertaining most of the work is done in advance, which allows you to spend time with your guests. The benefit for guests is they can choose what they would like to eat and in what combination.

**Stagger oven-cooked items** as overcrowding your oven changes cooking times.

**When serving food at room temperature** remember to keep it safe as food should be kept like this for a maximum of 2 hours. That leaves ample time for all to eat merrily and then move on to the desserts.

## Making ahead
Follow these very simple tips for getting ahead.

**Make extra.** When making some dishes, make extra so that you can serve some for dinner and store the rest. While there is sometimes a bit of extra work in doubling or tripling a recipe, it's rarely double or triple the effort.

**Keep it separate.** It's best to leave all components stored separately. Slow-cooked items can then be reheated gently and if serving with vegetables, they stay fresh and crisp. Having stackable plastic or glass containers helps with storage and when strapped for space freezer bags save space.

**Enliven with fresh ingredients.** Whether it is fresh herbs, a crisp salad, toasted nuts, shaved cheese or bright vegetables – a pre-made dish can be enlivened. Not only is it aesthetically appealing but it's great for texture and nutritional value.

# THE ELEMENTS OF A PERFECT PARTY

1. Setting the table and tips on how to keep everything fresh.

- Just to make life easier for you, set the table before your guests arrive, whether it's for a help-yourself buffet or a more formal setting. That includes glasses, napkins, salt and pepper and servingware.
- Food should be kept at ambient temperature for a maximum of 2 hours.
- For fresh ingredients such as salads, crudités and fruit, it is best to prep beforehand and store separately wrapped in clingfilm/plastic wrap and stored in airtight containers in the fridge. To maximize freshness, replenish in batches – there's no need to bring all the food out at once.
- The same goes for breads and dips – put out half and then top up. Nothing is worse than dried-out bread or crusty dips. Also, it's good to keep back some food just in case some of your guests are running late.

2. Creating a balance of raw, cooked and warmed food.

- The key to all these menus is the balance between raw, cooked ambient and warmed food. It is this balance that will create an interesting meal and keep you relaxed.
- Whether it's a starter, main or dessert, in most cases I like to introduce all these elements. It is also a relatively healthy way to eat. Vegetables are my biggest inspiration and to me they are the main event, with protein being on the side. Don't get me wrong – I love all protein, but eating, cooking and serving vegetables feels really nourishing.
- When setting one of these tables it is the vegetables that are generally the raw, cooked and warmed elements – of course there are warm meat and fish dishes, but the veggies do a lot of work. They are hard workers so celebrate them.

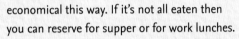

- If served raw, keep them crisp and fresh and, unless pre-washed, wash and thoroughly dry them.
- For the ambient cooked, again, serve in batches – in fact it's more economical this way. If it's not all eaten then you can reserve for supper or for work lunches.
- For warmed food – again, with these recipes I have tried to come up with dishes that are delicious warm but can also be eaten at room temperature. It is with these dishes that I like to serve fresh, crisp raw sides.

3. Decorating tips and making your tables and platters fun.

- The best decoration is getting the best quality ingredients you can get. Use them in an eye-catching salad, serve them as crudités or have a bowl of gorgeous vegetables or fruit – nothing is more beautiful. Decorations need not be extravagant, a hint of glam and elegance is great but not if it breaks the bank.
- To keep the gathering and the table relaxed, don't be tempted to overwhelm your guests with too many decorations. A pretty vase of flowers, a bowl of beautiful lemons, pots of fresh herbs or a few lovely succulents add an understated yet decorative touch. Let the food celebrate itself. A table that has mixed fruit with vegetables, pitchers of drinks, breads, nibbles, flowers, ambient food on platters and warmed food on boards and the company of your friends and family is a perfect gathering itself.

What's not to like about breakfast and brunch? Start
your day with a celebration – get up late, laze and gently
move into that late breakfast/early lunch. Mid-morning
tipples, easy feed-a-crowd dishes, things to make ahead
and show-stoppers are all to be found here.

# BREAKFAST
# & BRUNCH

# Naughty but nice breakfast

The best way to live your life is with a balance of naughty and nice. Where possible use the most unprocessed ingredients and methods when cooking, but just a touch of naughty won't kill you either. All these recipes are nourishing for your body and soul but do not skimp on flavour – we need to have fun, right?

## Menu

Green piña colada smoothie

Pomegranate & mint green tea

Glow balls

Grainy porridge

Sourdough toast toppings –

*Sweet* Whipped honey vanilla butter;

Tahini maple spread;

Crushed berries & goat's curd

*Savoury* Avocado & salmon;

Broad bean, courgette & goat's curd

Prosciutto eggs

Cauliflower, butternut & kale hash

Rhubarb mini cakes

## PARTY PLANNING

'Fresh is best' for most of the recipes in this menu, with a few exceptions.

*The day before:*
· Make the Glow balls and refrigerate.
· Whip the Honey vanilla butter. Make the Tahini maple spread and Crushed berries and refrigerate.
· Make the Rhubarb mini cakes and store in an airtight container.
· Weigh out the Grainy porridge except for the liquid ingredients and place in a saucepan.

*On the morning of the breakfast:*
· Make the Cauliflower, butternut & kale hash and the Broad bean, courgette & goat's curd mixture.
· Place the Green piña colada smoothie ingredients in the blender (but don't blend).
· Get the teapot ready but don't pour in the hot water.
· Cook the Grainy porridge and set aside to reheat when your guests arrive.

*One hour before:*
· Set up the food and drinks buffet-style, grouping the savoury and sweet dishes together.
· Make the Sourdough toasts and place on a wooden board or platter. Place all the extras on the buffet table.
· Make the Prosciutto eggs.

*When your guests arrive:*
· Blitz the Green piña colada smoothie, add the Malibu if your guests are in that type of mood and make the tea.
· Heat the porridge and place on the table. Gently heat the Cauliflower, butternut & kale hash and place with the Prosciutto eggs.
· Don't forget the Rhubarb mini cakes!

# Glow balls

Brazil nuts are an excellent source of complex B vitamins. With the addition of the power spice turmeric, cocoa nibs and bee pollen, these balls will have you glowing inside and out. Make a batch and freeze them. They are a perfect snack or a fun porridge topper.

**200 g/1½ cups Brazil nuts**
**100 g/¾ cup dates, pitted**
**100 g/¾ cup dried figs**
**1 tablespoon desiccated/dried unsweetened shredded coconut**
**2 tablespoons coconut oil**
**½ teaspoon ground turmeric**
**½ teaspoon ground cinnamon**
**4 cardamom pods, ground**
**2 tablespoons ground flax seeds**
**1 tablespoon cocoa nibs**
**½ tablespoon bee pollen**

MAKES 40 (TEASPOON SIZE)

In a food processor place the Brazil nuts, dates, figs, desiccated/ dried unsweetened shredded coconut, coconut oil, turmeric, cinnamon, cardamom and flax seeds and blitz into a textured paste. Transfer into a bowl and mix in the cocoa nibs and bee pollen. Form into 40 balls. Store in the fridge until needed.

# Grainy porridge

This is an earthier version of traditional porridge, made using ancient grains.

50 g/¼ cup quinoa
100 g/½ cup amaranth
100 g/½ cup millet
a pinch of salt
450 ml/scant 2 cups almond, coconut or oat milk of your choice, plus extra to serve

TO SERVE
almond, coconut or oat milk
bee pollen
pumpkin seeds
goji berries
nuts
honey
Glow balls (see left)
Whipped honey vanilla butter (see page 18)

MAKES 6 SMALL BOWLS
OR 3 LARGE BOWLS

Bring the quinoa, amaranth, millet, salt, non-dairy milk and 450 ml/ scant 2 cups water to the boil in a medium pan. Reduce the heat, partially cover and simmer, stirring occasionally, until the cereal is the consistency of porridge (softer and thicker than the usual bowl of oatmeal) and water is absorbed, approx. 40–50 minutes. If you want a looser, creamier texture, add more milk at this stage. Serve with your choice of the toppings, above.

## Make it pretty

Keep it natural, fresh and light.
Use wooden boards to serve
all the food and pots of fresh
herbs and ferns to decorate.

## Green piña colada smoothie

Tropical goodness in a glass –
or add a shot of Malibu to make
it really naughty!

**1 pineapple, peeled, cored and
roughly chopped
1 banana
juice of 1 lime
100 ml/scant ½ cup coconut milk
a large handful of spinach
ice cubes**

SERVES 6

Blitz all the ingredients together in
a blender for a smooth consistency.
Add Malibu for a dirty one. Pour
into six tall glasses and serve.

## Pomegranate & mint green tea

Green tea and ruby jewels to replenish and refresh you.

**3 green teabags**
**2 large sprigs of mint**
**50 ml/3½ tablespoons pomegranate juice**
**1 tablespoon pomegranate seeds (optional), plus a few extra to serve in each glass**

*6-cup teapot*

SERVES 6

Place the teabags and mint in the teapot. Boil enough water to fill the teapot, let it wait for 3 minutes, then pour into the teapot and allow to infuse for up to 3 minutes. Remove the teabags from the teapot, add the pomegranate juice and seeds (if using) and serve.

# Sourdough toast toppings

A brown rye sourdough works well with both sweet or savoury or – my favourite – somewhere in between. Buy a good sourdough from your local bakery and serve with the following toppings.

## Whipped honey vanilla butter

150 g/1¼ sticks salted butter, softened
1 teaspoon vanilla paste
2 tablespoons runny honey
bee pollen, to sprinkle

Place the softened butter, vanilla paste and honey in a bowl. Using a hand-held mixer, whisk the ingredients together until light and fluffy. Serve sprinkled with bee pollen.

## Crushed berries & goat's curd

500 g/3 cups frozen berries
2 tablespoons sugar
1 teaspoon vanilla paste
100 g/¾ cup goat's curd, to serve

Place the berries, sugar and vanilla paste in a saucepan and heat gently, crushing the berries with a fork. Do not overcook as you want to retain some texture. Serve with the goat's curd.

## Tahini maple spread

100 g/½ cup tahini
2 tablespoons maple syrup
1–2 tablespoons warm water
sesame seeds, to sprinkle

Place the tahini and maple syrup in a bowl and mix well. Add the warm water to loosen the spread. Sprinkle with sesame seeds and serve.

## Avocado & salmon

2–3 avocados, peeled, stoned/ pitted and sliced
200 g/1 cup smoked salmon
a handful of large capers
lemon, sliced, to serve

Assemble the ingredients on a large platter and allow your guests to top their own toast with the avocados, salmon, capers and a slice of lemon.

## Broad bean, courgette & goat's curd

1 tablespoon olive oil
1 courgette/zucchini, thinly sliced into half moons
2 spring onions/scallions, sliced
150 g/1¼ cups frozen broad/fava beans, defrosted and skins removed
a handful of parsley, finely chopped
a handful of chives, finely chopped
juice of ½ lemon
grated zest of 1 lemon
100 g/¾ cup goat's curd, to serve
sea salt and freshly ground black pepper

Heat the oil in a frying pan/ skillet. Add the courgette/ zucchini, spring onions/scallions and broad/fava beans. Cook for 10 minutes – they should be just cooked and retain some bite. Place in a bowl and finish with the herbs, lemon juice and zest, goat's curd and salt and pepper.

### *Maximize flavour*

Goat's curd is excellent for cooking, as it is wonderfully versatile. It can be used in sweet or savoury dishes in place of cream cheese, ricotta or quark. It has a fresh, clean flavour and a light, melt-in-the-mouth creamy texture.

## Prosciutto eggs

This is a cheat's fancy ham and egg and a nice way to serve it to a crowd.

**6 slices of prosciutto**
**6 eggs**
**6 sprigs of thyme**
**a handful of grated Parmesan (optional)**

*6-hole muffin pan, greased with vegetable oil*

MAKES 6

Preheat the oven to 200°C (400°F) Gas 6.

Line the prepared muffin pan with prosciutto and place in the preheated oven for 5 minutes. Using two spoons, pull the prosciutto back against the sides of the muffin holes. Crack an egg into each prosciutto-lined muffin hole and top with a sprig of thyme and a pinch of Parmesan. Bake for 10–15 minutes or until set. Remove from the oven and take out of their moulds.

## Cauliflower, butternut & kale hash

So delicious and good for you too! I eat the leftovers for supper with a poached egg and a dash of sriracha sauce for extra kick.

1 tablespoon olive oil
2 tablespoons butter
1 onion, roughly chopped
1 garlic clove, crushed
½ cauliflower, cut into bitesize pieces
150 g/5½ oz. butternut squash, peeled and cut into bitesize pieces
a handful of kale, stems removed, leaves roughly chopped
2 tablespoons finely chopped chives
grated Parmesan (optional)
sea salt and freshly ground black pepper

SERVES 6

In a large frying pan/skillet heat the olive oil and butter. Add the onion and garlic and cook for 5 minutes. Add the cauliflower and squash, season with salt and pepper and cook on a medium heat for 20 minutes, stirring regularly.

Add the kale and cook for a further 10 minutes. The pan should have enough space for each vegetable to colour really well, and if they catch a little – even better. Once cooked through and caramelized, check the seasoning and add salt and pepper if necessary. Top with the chives and Parmesan, if using, and serve.

# Rhubarb mini cakes

I love these cakes and always burn my mouth as I have to eat one as soon as it comes out of the oven. The spices, the sharpness of the rhubarb and the soft cake make a divine combination. The perfect alternative to stodgy muffins as the self-raising/rising flour and buttermilk produce a light texture.

150 g/5½ oz. rhubarb, roughly chopped into 2.5 cm/1 in. pieces
150 g/¾ cup brown sugar
250 g/1¾ cups self-raising/rising flour
1 teaspoon ground cinnamon
1 teaspoon ground ginger
2 eggs, lightly beaten
1 teaspoon vanilla paste
100 ml/scant ½ cup buttermilk
150 ml/⅔ cup vegetable oil
a handful of demerara sugar

*12 mini loaf (or muffin) pans, greased*

MAKES 12

Preheat the oven to 180°C (350°F) Gas 4.

Mix the rhubarb with 2 tablespoons of the brown sugar. This will start to draw out the moisture in the rhubarb and become a syrup. Leave for 10 minutes.

Place the flour, remaining brown sugar, cinnamon and ginger in a large bowl. Add the eggs, vanilla paste, buttermilk and oil, and mix until just combined. Gently stir the rhubarb through the mixture. Spoon into the mini loaf pans.

Top each with demerara sugar. Bake for 20 minutes in the preheated oven or until a skewer inserted into the centre comes out clean. Set aside to cool for 2 minutes in the pans before transferring to a wire rack to cool completely.

# Brunch bonanza

It's always nice catching up with friends and brunch is a great time to do it. The hours between breakfast and lunch are the perfect opportunity to mix sweet and savoury dishes. This menu is a combination of healthy food, such as granola, and more indulgent dishes, like the Breakfast tart washed down with a Pomini – a grapefruit Champagne cocktail. This whole menu works well as a lovely mid-morning meal, and then you have the rest of the day to get on with life or keep the party going.

Always feel free to experiment – any of these recipes could stand well on their own.

## Menu

Pomini

Quinoa granola, tropical fruit
& coconut yogurt

Sweet potato, pea & mint fritters

Avocado whip

Breakfast tart

Roasted cherry tomato chutney

Quick cornbread

Scorched ricotta with herbs & honey

## PARTY PLANNING

There's a fair amount of prep you can do ahead so that you're not working flat out in the morning.

*In advance:*
· The Quinoa granola can be made in advance and stored for weeks. The cornbread can be made ahead and frozen (defrost on the morning of your brunch).

*The night before:*
· Make the leek mix for the Breakfast tart ahead.
· Prep the Sweet potato, pea & mint fritters.
· Make the Roasted cherry tomato chutney (it actually gets better with time).

*The morning (obviously early – but that's what you do for those that you love):*
· Prep the Breakfast tart and Avocado whip and set aside.

*When your guests arrive:*
· Serve everyone with a Pomini.
· Refresh the cornbread in the oven.
· Gently heat the fritters in a hot oven in one layer on a parchment-lined baking sheet. Serve them with the Roasted cherry tomato chutney, Avocado whip and Quick cornbread.
· Serve the Granola, fruit and yogurt.
· Finish off the Breakfast tart and serve.
· Turn the grill/broiler on to scorch the ricotta and serve alongside the Quick cornbread drizzled with honey. Enjoy your guests' company and then the rest of the day.

*Make it pretty*

Place some vibrant pretty flowers and colourful linen on the table to brighten up the day.

## Pomini

The tartness of the grapefruit juice works well with the Champagne as a refreshing brunch cocktail, kickstarting your appetite.

**300 ml/1¼ cups grapefruit juice**
**1 bottle Champagne (750 ml/ 3 cups)**
**1 small grapefruit, cut into 6 small slices**

SERVES 6

Divide the grapefruit juice between six Champagne glasses and top with Champagne. Add a slice of grapefruit and serve.

# Quinoa granola, tropical fruit & coconut yogurt

A nourishing gluten- and refined sugar-free granola, served on coconut yogurt with fruit.

150 g/1 cup quinoa granola (see below)

150 g/3½ oz. (about ¼) papaya, washed and cut into shards

150 g/3½ oz. pineapple, peeled, cored and cut into shards

150 g/3½ oz. mango, washed and cut into shards

2 passion fruits, halved

200 g/1 cup coconut milk yogurt, such as Coyo

coconut blossom syrup, to serve

GRANOLA

200 g/2 cups quinoa flakes

2 tablespoons ground flaxseeds

1 tablespoon chia seeds (optional)

50 g/scant ½ cup macadamia nuts, roughly chopped

50 g/scant ½ cup pistachio nuts, roughly chopped

50 g/scant ½ cup cashew nuts, roughly chopped

4 tablespoons coconut blossom syrup

1 tablespoon apple juice

1 teaspoon vanilla paste

30 g/¾ cup coconut chips, lightly toasted

*baking sheet lined with parchment paper*

SERVES 6

Preheat the oven to 180°C (350°F) Gas 4.

Put the quinoa flakes, ground flaxseeds, chia seeds (if using) and the nuts in a large bowl and mix together. Stir in the coconut blossom syrup, apple juice and vanilla paste. Spread the mixture onto the prepared baking sheet and bake in the preheated oven for 10 minutes. Break up the mixture with a fork and bake for another 10 minutes. Remove from the oven and stir in the coconut chips. Allow to cool. Store in an airtight container for up to a month (this keeps well so you may wish to double up on the quantities).

Arrange the fruit on a serving platter and place a bowl of the coconut yogurt, a jar of granola and a little pot of coconut blossom syrup alongside for people to help themselves.

# Sweet potato, pea & mint fritters

Not only can these fritters be served at brunch, but they're also brilliant as a side dish with meat, poultry or fish for dinner or in a wrap with salad for lunch.

2 eggs
1 sweet potato, peeled, grated and squeezed of moisture
80 g/½ cup petit pois
2 spring onions/ scallions, chopped
3 tablespoons plain/ all-purpose flour

4 sprigs of mint, leaves removed and chopped
1 tablespoon olive oil
sea salt and freshly ground black pepper
coconut oil, for frying

MAKES 10–12

Whisk the eggs well in a small bowl. Combine with the sweet potato, peas, spring onions/scallions, flour, mint, olive oil and salt and pepper to taste, mixing well.

In a large pan, melt the coconut oil over a medium heat. Spoon in the potato mixture, 1 heaping tablespoon at a time, and pat down into a flat patty with a spatula. Cook for 4 minutes on each side until golden and crispy. Remove from the pan with a spatula, drain on paper towels and serve.

## Avocado whip

This avo whip has a smoothness to it and works nicely as a dip. For a much creamier and fluffier consistency, use a Nutribullet-type blender – it's worth it. But if you are in the more chunky avo brigade, coarsely chop all the ingredients instead.

2 avocados, peeled and stoned/pitted
a handful of spinach
a handful of parsley
juice of 1 lemon
30 ml/2 tablespoons olive oil
sea salt and freshly ground black pepper

SERVES 6

In a food processor, blitz the avocado, spinach, parsley, lemon juice, olive oil and salt and pepper into a smooth, light and fluffy paste. Transfer to a bowl to serve.

# Breakfast tart

When constructing this tart, it is important to create a good dam, or well, for the egg to sit in to prevent any spillages. When you arrange the first layer of leeks, create the wells and reinforce them with the pancetta – serious building skills are required here!

50 g/3½ tablespoons butter, roughly chopped
1 leek, thinly sliced
1 garlic clove, finely chopped
2 tablespoons roughly chopped thyme and oregano (alternatively use 1 teaspoon each of dried thyme and oregano)

8 filo/phyllo pastry sheets
10 slices pancetta
6 eggs, at room temperature
1 tablespoon olive oil
1½ handfuls of rocket/arugula, coarsely chopped

20 x 29 cm/8 x 11½ in. baking sheet

SERVES 4–6

Preheat the oven to 180°C (350°F) Gas 4.

Melt half the butter in a large frying pan/skillet over a medium heat, add the leek and garlic and stir occasionally until starting to caramelize (approx. 6–7 minutes). Add the herbs to the pan and set aside off the heat.

Melt the remaining butter and brush the base and sides of the baking sheet. Trim the filo/phyllo pastry sheets to fit the inside the baking sheet. Place the first pastry sheet on the baking sheet, brush with butter, then lay over another pastry sheet and repeat until all the pastry is used.

Spread the leek mixture over the pastry base. Make six evenly spaced indentations in the leek mixture. Place the pancetta over the tart, leaving the indentations free for the eggs. Place in the preheated oven for 7 minutes.

Crack the eggs into the indentations, drizzle with oil and bake until the tart is set and the eggs are medium cooked (approx. 10–15 minutes). Scatter over the rocket/arugula and return to the oven until just wilted. Serve with the Roasted cherry tomato chutney (see below).

# Roasted cherry tomato chutney

A very versatile, delicious and easy-to-make sweet and savoury tomato chutney. It tastes better the day after it has been made and if you do have any left over, it's great in a sandwich with ham and lettuce.

500 g/3 cups cherry tomatoes, halved
2 tablespoons olive oil
1 red onion, finely chopped
2 garlic cloves, crushed
50 ml/3½ tablespoons apple cider vinegar
1 teaspoon white mustard seeds

2 tablespoons brown sugar
½ teaspoon chilli/hot red pepper flakes
a pinch of dried curry leaves
1 bay leaf
sea salt

SERVES 6 AS A SIDE

Preheat the oven to 180°C (350°F) Gas 4.

Place all the ingredients in a shallow baking pan, drizzle with the oil, cover and roast in the preheated oven for 50 minutes until they are soft, tossing occasionally to avoid sticking. Uncover the pan, increase the temperature to 200°C (400°F) Gas 6 and return to the oven to caramelize for approx. 10–15 minutes. Leave to cool before serving. Enjoy with just about anything you like.

## Quick cornbread

Quick and easy, this is a bread that can be made in advance and frozen.
Perfect served with both sweet and savoury accompaniments.

150 g/1 heaping cup plain/
   all-purpose flour
3 teaspoons baking powder
1 teaspoon salt
170 g/1 heaping cup cornmeal
1 teaspoon caster/granulated
   sugar
1 teaspoon smoked paprika
250 ml/1 cup milk
leaves from 4 sprigs of oregano,
   plus a little extra to sprinkle
   over the top before cooking

160 g/1 heaping cup canned
   sweetcorn/corn kernels,
   reserving a tablespoon
   to sprinkle over the top
   before cooking
60 ml/¼ cup olive oil
1 egg, lightly whisked
honey, to drizzle

*13 x 24 cm/5 x 10 in. loaf pan,
greased with olive oil and lightly
dusted with flour*

MAKES 1 LOAF

Preheat the oven to 220°C
(425°F) Gas 7.

In a large bowl mix together
all the ingredients and pour the
mixture into the prepared pan.
Bake in the preheated oven for
30–35 minutes or until a skewer
inserted into the centre comes
out clean. Set aside to cool for
5 minutes before turning out
onto a wire rack. Serve warm or
at room temperature, drizzled
with honey.

## Scorched ricotta with herbs & honey

I just love this dish. It's so simple, but so impressive – the best things always are.

**225 g/1 cup ricotta cheese**
**4 sprigs of thyme**
**sea salt and freshly ground black pepper**
**30 ml/2 tablespoons runny honey**

SERVES 6

Preheat the oven to 180°C (350°F) Gas 4. Preheat the grill/broiler to a high temperature.

Place the ricotta, thyme, salt and pepper in an ovenproof dish with the runny honey drizzled over. Place the ricotta under the grill/broiler and allow to scorch and the honey to caramelize – this should take 5–10 minutes, depending how hot the grill/broiler is, so keep an eye on it. Once you have achieved a scorched colour, move the dish to the preheated oven and bake for a further 10 minutes. Serve warm.

Quick brunch
for a bunch

This is a collection of natural and easy breakfast recipes that go really well together, but you can also mix and match them. You can make just two or three of them if you are in a hurry, or all of them if you have the time. Keeping a batch of the Spelt, banana & chocolate muffins and the Spinach triangles in the freezer is a good start.

## Menu

Lemongrass & cucumber, Citrus
& Strawberry & basil flavoured waters

Blackberry & blueberry açai bowl

Kale & sweet potato frittata

Buttered mushrooms

Spinach triangles

Spelt, banana & chocolate muffins

Gluten-free apple pancakes

# PARTY PLANNING

*A week or so before:*
· Make the Spelt, banana & chocolate muffins and freeze. Prepare the Spinach triangles, don't bake and freeze.

*On the morning of the breakfast:*
· Defrost the Spelt, banana & chocolate muffins.
· Bake the Spinach triangles from frozen.
· Make the Kale & sweet potato frittata and the Buttered mushrooms.
· Make the flavoured waters.

*As your guests arrive:*
· Blitz the Blackberry & blueberry açai smoothie bowl and serve.
· Serve the Kale & sweet potato frittata and Buttered mushrooms.
· Bring out the Spelt, banana & chocolate muffins and Spinach triangles.
· Make the Gluten-free apple pancakes and serve.
· Enjoy everyone's company and crack on with your day.

# Flavoured waters

Be creative and come up with exciting variations of flavoured water. These are some of my favourites. The addition of iced edible flowers brings an ethereal touch.

## Lemongrass & cucumber

**2 lemongrass stalks, bruised**
**1 small cucumber, thinly pared**
**ice**
**1.5 litres/6 cups water (or enough to fill the jug/pitcher)**

SERVES 6

Mix the lemongrass, cucumber, ice and water in a jug/pitcher and serve.

## Citrus

**¼ grapefruit, thinly sliced**
**1 lemon, thinly sliced**
**ice**
**1.5 litres/6 cups water (or enough to fill the jug/pitcher)**

SERVES 6

Mix the citrus fruit, ice and water in a jug/pitcher and serve.

# Blackberry & blueberry açai bowl

As a food, açai pulp from the tribal Amazon belt is often blended with the starchy root vegetable manioc and eaten as porridge. The taste is often described as reminiscent of wild berries and chocolate. The addition of it in powdered form in a smoothie and blended with fresh berries gives you a great start to the day.

200 ml/scant 1 cup
  coconut water
2 ripe bananas (if you
  have a Nutribullet,
  you could put them
  chopped into the
  freezer and add them
  straight from there
  for a creamier
  texture)
100 g/½ cup frozen
  blueberries
50 g/¼ cup frozen
  blackberries
1 tablespoon açai
  powder
1 tablespoon oats,
  gluten free if you
  wish, to make it a bit
  thicker and creamier
  (optional)

TO SERVE
100 g/¾ cup
  blueberries
50 g/⅓ cup blackberries
1 dragon fruit, cleaned
  and sliced
50 g/⅓ cup kiwiberries
  or 1 whole kiwi,
  cleaned and sliced
1 tablespoon slivered
  pistachios
a few sprigs of mint

SERVES 4 IN
SMALL BOWLS

Blend the coconut water, bananas, frozen berries and açai powder together in a blender until smooth. Stand for a few minutes to thicken. Spoon into 4 small serving bowl. Arrange the fresh fruit, pistachios and mint on top and serve.

## Strawberry & basil

5 strawberries, hulled and quartered
a bunch of basil
ice
1.5 litres/6 cups water (or enough
  to fill the jug/pitcher)

SERVES 6

Mix the strawberries, basil, ice and water in a jug/pitcher and serve.

## *Make it pretty*

Sometimes simplicity is the key. Keep it light with a linen tablecloth and let the food be the decoration. The flavoured water jugs/pitchers will add beauty to the table, as do the edible flowers.

# Kale & sweet potato frittata

This is a wholesome superfood frittata and can also be served for dinner or a light lunch. For breakfast it will set you up for the day.

1 tablespoon olive oil
2 red onions, thinly sliced
1 sweet potato, scrubbed and thinly sliced into rounds
1 beetroot/beet
8 eggs
100 g/3 cups chopped curly kale
1 tablespoon balsamic vinegar
2 garlic cloves, crushed
100 g/½ cup ricotta
4 sprigs of lemon thyme, leaves picked, plus 3 extra for decorating the top
sea salt and freshly ground black pepper

25 cm/10 in. ovenproof frying pan/skillet

SERVES 4

Preheat the oven to 190°C (375°F) Gas 5.

Heat the oil in the frying pan/skillet. Add the onions and cook for 10–15 minutes until soft and caramelized.

Meanwhile, place the sweet potato in a pan of water, bring to the boil and cook for approx. 8 minutes. Drain and allow to dry out, and season with salt and pepper.

Place the whole beetroot/beet in another pan with water, bring to the boil and cook for 15 minutes. Drain and allow to cool, then peel and thinly slice on a mandoline.

Whisk the eggs in a bowl and season.

Add the kale and 1 tablespoon of water to the onion mixture and cook for 5 minutes until the kale has wilted. Add the balsamic vinegar and garlic and let bubble for 1 minute; if it becomes too sticky just add a touch of water to loosen the mixture.

Next, add the sweet potato, beetroot/beet and eggs. Give everything a quick stir, then leave undisturbed to cook over a low-medium heat for 5 minutes until the egg is nearly set and the frittata is turning golden brown on the bottom.

Dot the ricotta and lemon thyme around the frittata. Cook in the preheated oven for 10–15 minutes until the cheese is bubbling and the frittata is set in the centre.

# Buttered mushrooms

The creaminess of the mushrooms combined with the sharp and tangy lemony sauce make a great side dish to the Kale & sweet potato frittata. These are also brilliant piled on top of toast.

400 g/5 cups mixed mushrooms
60 g/½ stick unsalted butter
1 banana shallot or small onion, thinly sliced
2 garlic cloves, thinly sliced
grated zest of 1 lemon
juice of ½ lemon
½ bunch of flat-leaf parsley, roughly chopped (optional)
2–3 sprigs of lemon thyme
buttered, toasted baguettes and extra lemon wedges, to serve

SERVES 4 AS A SIDE

Brush the mushrooms clean, halve the larger ones and set aside. Heat the butter in a large frying pan/skillet over a medium-high heat until foaming. Add the shallot and garlic and cook for approx. 4–5 minutes, until soft. Add the mushrooms and cook, stirring, for another 4–5 minutes, until just tender. Add the lemon zest and juice and herbs and season to taste. Serve with buttered toasted baguettes and lemon wedges.

# Spinach triangles

An all-time family favourite of mine. I always have a batch of these in the freezer and they can be eaten – as they do in Greece – for breakfast, as a snack or at any time of the day.

2 teaspoons olive oil
100 g/3½ oz. baby spinach, trimmed and chopped
100 g/¾ cup feta, crumbled
½ bunch of dill, finely chopped
½ bunch of parsley, finely chopped
½ teaspoon freshly grated nutmeg
9 sheets filo/phyllo pastry
125 g/1⅛ stick butter, melted
1 tablespoon nigella seeds
sea salt and freshly ground black pepper

*2 large baking sheets lined with parchment paper*

MAKES 9

Preheat the oven to 180°C (350°F) Gas 4.

Heat the oil in a large frying pan/skillet over a medium-high heat. Add the spinach and cook for 4–5 minutes or until wilted. Transfer to a colander and let cool for 10 minutes, then roughly chop and squeeze out excess water. Place the spinach in a large bowl and stir in the feta and herbs. Season with salt, pepper and nutmeg.

Place a pastry sheet on a flat surface. Brush with butter. Top with another pastry sheet, brush with butter, top with a third pastry sheet. Cut into 3 long strips. Cover the remaining pastry with damp kitchen towel.

Place 1 tablespoon of the spinach mixture in one corner of pastry. Fold over diagonally to form a triangle. Continue folding, retaining the triangle shape. Place on the baking sheet. Repeat with the remaining 2 strips, then repeat with the rest of the pastry, butter and spinach mixture. Brush with the remaining butter and scatter over nigella seeds. Bake in the preheated oven for 25 minutes or until golden and crisp.

# Spelt, banana & chocolate muffins

These are earthy, sweet and chocolatey. Ditch your traditional stodgy muffins for this lighter version. They can be made ahead and frozen – they also make the perfect afternoon tea treat.

1 teaspoon baking powder
1 teaspoon bicarbonate of soda/ baking soda
a pinch of salt
150 g/1¼ sticks unsalted butter, softened at room temperature
250 g/1¼ cups soft brown sugar
2 eggs, lightly beaten
2 very ripe bananas, mashed with a fork
100 g/½ cup Greek yogurt
230 g/1¾ cups spelt flour
60 g/½ cup dark chocolate chips
cocoa powder, to serve

*12-hole muffin pan lined with muffin cases*

MAKES 12

Preheat the oven to 170°C (325°F) Gas 3.

Place all the ingredients apart from the spelt flour and chocolate chips in a food processor and pulse until smooth, the add the spelt flour and chocolate chips by hand and gently mix.

Transfer the mixture to the prepared muffin pan and make sure to fill only three-quarters full.

Bake in the preheated oven for 25–30 minutes, or until the muffins are firm and golden brown. Cool in the pan for 10 minutes before turning out onto a wire rack to cool completely. Serve dusted with cocoa powder.

# Gluten-free apple pancakes

These are quick to make and will be enjoyed by everyone, not just your gluten-free guests. The combination of the light nuttiness of the buckwheat, the tartness of the apple and the mellow sweetness of the maple syrup is a winner.

150 g/1 heaping cup gluten-free plain/all-purpose flour
100 g/¾ cup buckwheat flour
1 tablespoon caster/granulated sugar
1 teaspoon gluten-free baking powder
a pinch of salt
1 egg
220 ml/scant 1 cup milk
½ teaspoon vanilla paste
butter, for frying
1 Granny Smith apple, cored, peeled and sliced into circles
maple syrup, yogurt, vanilla powder and blackberries, to serve

SERVES 4 ( MAKES 2–3 SMALL PANCAKES EACH)

Put the flours, sugar, baking powder and salt in a bowl and make a well in the centre. Crack the egg in the middle and pour in one-quarter of the milk. Use a whisk to combine the mixture thoroughly. Once you have a paste, mix in another quarter of the milk and, when all the lumps are gone, mix in the remaining milk and the vanilla paste. Leave to rest for 20 minutes. Stir again before cooking.

Heat a small non-stick frying pan/skillet and add a knob/pat of butter. When the butter starts to foam, ladle the pancake mixture into the centre of the pan forming a circle, then place an apple ring in the centre. Cook for a few minutes until golden brown on the bottom and the bubbles are bursting on the surface of the pancake, then turn over and cook until golden on the other side. Repeat until you have used all the mixture, stirring the mixture between pancakes and adding more butter for frying as necessary.

Serve with maple syrup, yogurt, vanilla powder and blackberries.

*Maximize flavour*

Freshly ground vanilla powder is aromatic and flavourful. It can be purchased in most supermarkets. Alternatively, dry roast a vanilla pod/bean and blitz it in a food processor.

If you love sharing a long lunch with your friends and family, then a graze-all-day table is the best recipe. You want guests to relax and linger and they will go where the action is – besides, they want to hang out with the host. A mixture of hot and cold food, good drink and relaxed decorating works best.

# LUNCH

# Menu

Watermelon fizzy punch

Blue cheese dip with rainbow crudités

Olive, parmesan & thyme breadsticks

Artichokes with pink peppercorn
vinaigrette

Tomato, tarragon & onion
roasted chicken

Baked mini courgettes with
goat's curd

Pan crisp new potatoes

Coconut pavlova with chocolate swirl
cream & cherries

# Relaxed roast

This is the perfect type of roast; one that can be eaten warm or at room temperature. It can be transported and the baked tomatoes are a lovely accompaniment. The use of tarragon, with its hints of aniseed and vanilla, always works well with chicken but when combined with tomatoes it's a revelation. This menu is a casual and easy way to use the best of what summer has to offer. A meal with friends and family should be a relaxed affair and with some tips and tricks you can get ahead and spend more time with those you love.

# PARTY PLANNING

*A week or so ahead:*
· Start making the Olive, parmesan & thyme breadsticks in advance and freeze them. Defrost on the morning of your lunch and you'll ensure maximum freshness. If time is really of the essence, then buy breadsticks and make all the other recipes.

*The night before:*
· Make the Coconut pavlova. A pavlova is best when cooked and left in the oven to cool overnight.
· Place the tarragon butter under the skin of the chicken and prepare all the other ingredients, cover well and refrigerate so they are ready to go into the oven.

*The morning of the lunch:*
· Cook the potatoes and place in a pan with the other ingredients, ready to be pan-fried.
· Place the courgettes/zucchini on a baking sheet and cover to keep fresh.
· Make the vinaigrette for the artichokes and set aside.
· Set the table – make sure you keep it relaxed.

*One and a half hours before your guests arrive:*
· Turn the oven on.
· Make the blue cheese dip and prepare the crudités – keep them covered with a clean, damp paper towel to keep them fresh.
· Make the watermelon mixture ready to be topped with prosecco for the punch.

*Half an hour before your guests arrive:*
· Place the chicken in the oven and cook the artichokes.

*When your guests arrive:*
· Make and serve the Watermelon fizzy punch and make sure to pour yourself one too!

· Place the dip and crudités on the table.
· When the artichokes are ready, serve them with the vinaigrette. Bring out the breadsticks and place them on the table.
· When the chicken is nearly ready, finish off the potatoes and bring the courgettes/zucchini to the table. When the chicken is done, serve it in the pan with the tomatoes as the sauce, and with the pan-fried potatoes.

*A couple more things:*
· Melt the chocolate and whip the cream, decorate the pavlova and serve.
· This is a shared chilled zone so ask for help – clear up together!

# Blue cheese dip with rainbow crudités

This dip is surprisingly light and savoury, making it the perfect accompaniment to crisp and crunchy vegetables.

### BLUE CHEESE DIP

- 150 g/¾ cup Greek yogurt
- 150 g/¾ cup ricotta
- ½ teaspoon chopped chives, reserving some to finish
- juice of ½ lemon
- 100 g/¾ cup plus 2 tablespoons blue cheese (such as Roquefort or Stilton), crumbled
- 2–3 drops Worcestershire sauce, to taste

SERVES 6

### CRUDITÉS

- 6 green beans (approx. 50 g/⅓ cup), blanched and cooled
- 6–10 (approx. 100 g/ 1 cup) asparagus spears, very lightly blanched and cooled
- 1 yellow (bell) pepper, cut into batons
- 1 head chicory, leaves separated
- 3–4 baby topped carrots, peeled and halved lengthways
- 3 mini cucumbers, cut into batons
- 1 bunch of radishes, washed and green leaves kept

First make the dip. Put the Greek yogurt, ricotta, chives and lemon juice in a bowl and mix well. Add the crumbled blue cheese, making sure it stays quite lumpy. Drizzle with 2–3 drops of Worcestershire sauce, to taste.

Place the bowl on a platter and surround with all the crudités – at this stage you can cover with clingfilm/plastic wrap and keep chilled until your guests arrive. To serve, scatter over the reserved chopped chives.

# Watermelon fizzy punch

This drink has a natural sweetness, but the addition of cucumber and lime keeps it tasting fresh. For teetotal guests, just add soda water instead of prosecco.

- 1 small watermelon (approx. 800 g/28 oz.), cut into chunks, skin and seeds removed
- 3 small cucumbers, 1 chopped for the juice and 2 thinly sliced lengthways
- 1 small bunch of mint, reserving some leaves to garnish
- 1 pink grapefruit, ½ for juice and ½ sliced into 6 rounds
- 3 limes, 1 sliced in rounds and 2 juiced
- 30 ml/2 tablespoons light agave syrup
- 1 bottle prosecco (750ml/3 cups)
- ice

SERVES 6

Put the chopped watermelon, one chopped cucumber and the mint leaves in a blender and blend together. Strain through a sieve/strainer into a jug/pitcher.

Put one slice each of grapefruit, lime and cucumber into each glass. Place the remaining sliced ingredients in the jug/pitcher and add the grapefruit juice, lime juice and agave syrup. Mix well. Top the pitcher and/or glasses with ice. Fill the pitcher with the prosecco and top with extra mint.

# Olive, parmesan & thyme breadsticks

Make a batch of these and freeze half for your next lunch. These breadsticks are so versatile flavourwise — try spreading them with pesto or harissa paste for some spicy heat.

500 g/3½ cups strong white bread flour, plus extra for dusting

10 g/2 teaspoons salt

10 g/1 tablespoon dried active yeast

350 ml/1½ cups tepid water (plus a little extra if needed)

2 tablespoons olive oil, plus extra for oiling

200 g/2 cups mixed black and green pitted olives in brine, drained

30 g/½ cup Parmesan, grated finely, plus extra for sprinkling

9 sprigs of thyme, leaves picked

fine semolina, for dusting

*3 baking sheets lined with parchment paper*

MAKES 12

Put the flour into the bowl of a mixer fitted with a dough hook. Add the salt to one side of the bowl and the yeast to the other. Add three-quarters of the water and begin mixing on a slow speed. As the dough starts to come together, add the remaining water gradually, approx. 50 ml/3½ tablespoons water at a time. Mix for a further 5–8 minutes on a medium speed. The dough should now be wet and stretch easily when pulled. Add the olive oil and mix for a further 2 minutes. Add the olives, half the Parmesan and the thyme leaves and mix until well distributed.

If freezing, place the dough in a lightly oiled freezable container or bag and put straight into the freezer. To defrost, leave the dough overnight in the fridge. When defrosted, remove from the container, place in a bowl and continue as below.

Cover the bowl with greased clingfilm/plastic wrap and allow to rise for 1 hour.

Preheat the oven to 200°C (400°F) Gas 6.

Dust the work surface heavily with flour and semolina and carefully tip out the dough. Do not knock back/punch down the dough – handle gently to keep as much air in the dough as possible. Dust the top of the dough with flour and stretch it out gently to a rough rectangle and top with the remaining Parmesan. Starting at one long edge, cut the dough into 12 strips (or 6 if using half the dough). Stretch each piece out until 20 cm/8 in. long, gently fold in half and twist evenly. Divide the breadsticks between the baking sheets, spacing them apart. Bake for 10–20 minutes until golden. Cool on a wire rack. Sprinkle with extra Parmesan.

# Artichokes with pink peppercorn vinaigrette

An elegant and classic dish, but so much fun to share.

6 globe artichokes, stalks removed
1 lemon, halved

VINAIGRETTE
120 ml/½ cup extra virgin olive oil
juice of ½ lemon
40 ml/3 tablespoons apple cider vinegar
1 teaspoon Dijon mustard
1 teaspoon runny honey
½ garlic clove
a small bunch of chives, finely chopped, to serve
1 teaspoon crushed pink peppercorns, to serve

*sterilized glass jar with a lid (see page 4)*

SERVES 6

To make the vinaigrette, put the olive oil, lemon juice, apple cider vinegar, mustard, honey and garlic in a blender and mix until emulsified. Using a blender will really emulsify the sauce and make it a perfectly creamy and thick dipping sauce. Pour into the glass jar. At this point you can store half of the dressing in the fridge for up to 2 weeks. Place the remaining dressing in a serving bowl and mix in the chopped chives and crushed pink peppercorns.

Bring a large pan of salted water to the boil with the lemon halves. Drop the artichokes into the water and place a small plate on top of them to weigh them down. Boil the artichokes for 40–45 minutes. When they're ready, you'll be able to pull a leaf out of the artichokes with no resistance.

To eat, pull off a leaf, dip the broken end into the vinaigrette, eat this and discard the rest. When you reach the middle, lift out the central leaves, scrape away the hairy choke and eat the artichoke heart.

# Tomato, tarragon & onion roasted chicken

This is great served warm or at room temperature, but it's equally delicious cold. Smoothing tarragon butter under the bird's skin helps to baste the chicken, and the herbs add a delicious flavour to the tomato sauce.

1 whole chicken (about 1.6 kg/ 3½ lb.)
500 g/18 oz. mixed tomatoes, halved
2 red onions, cleaned and cut into wedges
1 lemon, coarsely chopped
1 head garlic, halved horizontally
5 tarragon stalks
8 sprigs of thyme, plus extra leaves to serve
1 teaspoon honey
a pinch of chilli/red pepper flakes
2 tablespoons extra virgin olive oil
sea salt and freshly ground black pepper

TARRAGON BUTTER
60 g/½ stick salted butter, coarsely chopped, at room temperature
finely grated zest of 1 lemon
2 tablespoons finely chopped tarragon

SERVES 6

For the tarragon butter, mix the butter, lemon zest and chopped tarragon together in a bowl, then set aside.

Preheat the oven to 200°C (400°F) Gas 6.

Slide your fingers carefully between the skin and the breast of the chicken to separate, then loosen as much of the skin around the legs as possible without piercing the skin. Spoon two-thirds of the tarragon butter between the skin and the flesh and massage to distribute evenly. Spread the remaining tarragon butter over the chicken breast and thighs and set aside.

Take one of the halved tomatoes and stuff it into the chicken cavity with one onion, the chopped lemon, half of the garlic, one stalk of tarragon and the thyme sprigs. Tie the legs with kitchen twine and place the chicken in a roasting pan. Add the remaining tomatoes, onion, garlic and tarragon to the roasting pan, drizzle with the honey and add the pinch of chilli/red pepper flakes. Drizzle the chicken with olive oil and season.

Roast in the preheated oven, basting with the pan juices, for approx. 1 hour–1 hour 10 minutes until the skin is crisp and golden and the chicken is cooked through and the juices run clear. Serve at room temperature with Pan crisp new potatoes.

*Maximize flavour*

*Tarragon butter* – when making this recipe, double the quantity and freeze half. You then have a batch if you make the chicken again or you can serve it melted over a piece of steak or use it in a cheese and ham toastie.

# Baked mini courgettes with goat's curd

A very fresh, light and simple side, perfect served at room temperature.

**8 mini courgettes/ zucchini, halved**
**2 tablespoons olive oil**
**a pinch of chilli/red pepper flakes**
**100 g/½ cup goat's curd (or crumbled goat's cheese)**

**grated zest of 1 lemon**
**sea salt and freshly ground black pepper**

SERVES 6 AS A SIDE

Preheat the oven to 180°C (350°F) Gas 4.

Place the courgette/zucchini halves on a baking sheet and drizzle with olive oil, season with salt, pepper and chilli/red pepper flakes and bake in the preheated oven for 15 minutes. Top the courgettes/zucchini with the goat's curd and lemon zest and bake for a further 5 minutes. Serve warm or at room temperature.

# Pan crisp new potatoes

Once you have tried these, you'll find yourself serving them with most roasts. So easy and delicious.

**800 g/1¾ lb. mini new potatoes, scrubbed (unpeeled)**
**30 g/¼ stick unsalted butter**
**2 tablespoons olive oil**

**3 sprigs of thyme**
**sea salt and freshly ground black pepper**

SERVES 6 AS A SIDE

Bring a large pan of salted water to the boil. Add the potatoes and boil for 20 minutes or until cooked through, strain and return to the pan. At this stage you can set them aside until just before you serve.

Just before serving, add the butter, olive oil and thyme to the potatoes. Heat the pan on a medium heat and keep turning the potatoes until evenly browned and crispy. Season with sea salt and freshly ground pepper.

# Coconut pavlova with chocolate swirl cream & cherries

**MERINGUE**

**4 egg whites**

**250 g/1¼ cups golden caster/superfine sugar**

**1 teaspoon lemon juice**

**1 teaspoon cornflour/ cornstarch**

**1 teaspoon vanilla paste**

**100 g/1⅓ cups desiccated/dried unsweetened shredded coconut**

**TOPPING**

**400 ml/1¾ cups double/heavy cream**

**½ teaspoon vanilla paste**

**2 tablespoons icing/ confectioner's sugar**

**100 g/3½ oz. dark/ bittersweet chocolate, melted**

**1 punnet cherries**

**1 tablespoon coconut chips (optional)**

*baking sheet lined with parchment paper*

SERVES 8–10

Preheat the oven to 150°C (300°F) Gas 2.

Whisk the egg whites in a mixer until they form stiff peaks, then whisk in the sugar, 1 tablespoon at a time, until the meringue mixture looks glossy. Whisk in the lemon juice, cornflour/cornstarch and vanilla paste. Using a spoon, fold in the coconut. Spread the meringue in the centre of the prepared baking sheet into a circle approx. 23 cm/9 in. diameter, creating a crater in the middle. Bake in the preheated oven for 1 hour, then turn off the heat and let the pavlova cool completely inside the oven.

When the meringue is cool, whip the cream with the vanilla paste and icing/confectioner's sugar. Swirl in the melted chocolate but do not incorporate completely – 2–3 turns with the spoon is enough. Spread it over the meringue, drizzle over any remaining chocolate and top with cherries. Finish with the coconut chips, if using.

This cherry ripe-inspired pavlova,
with the combination of cherries,
chocolate and coconut, is always
a crowd pleaser! It can be made
in advance but always add the
toppings just before you serve.
It also works well with
strawberries if cherries
are not in season.

# Vegetable fiesta

Vegetables at any time of the year are beautiful, but winter
is my favourite time to eat them. This menu is vegetarian luxe
and although altogether it's a substantial and heartwarming
meal, you could always swap a recipe out for a roast chicken
if you wanted to offer the carnivores an option. Quite a few of
these dishes can be made in advance with just some last-minute
touches for the fresh additions. Let's keep this as easy as possible,
plan a little, then have a lot of fun.

## Menu

Blood orange & rosemary negronis

Santorini fava with griddled radicchio
& little gem lettuce wedges

Simple butternut & greens

Orecchiette with brussels sprouts
& burnt butter

Watercress falafel with grapefruit
& sumac yogurt

Winter root veg minestrone

Chocolate mud cake with whisky
& blood orange cream

Crispy blood oranges

## PARTY PLANNING

*A few days before:*
· Make the minestrone until the point where you need to add the green vegetables and refrigerate.
· Make the Santorini fava and refrigerate.
· Make the Chocolate mud cake, glaze and refrigerate.
· Make the chilli oil.

*The night before:*
· Make the Watercress falafel and store.
· Make the Crispy blood oranges.

*In the morning:*
· Get the elements ready for the Simple butternut & greens by roasting the butternut squash.
· Roast the Brussels sprouts and set aside.
· Prepare the tahini and grapefruit dressing.
· Make the Whisky & blood orange cream.

*One hour before:*
· Make the negroni pitcher and store in the fridge.
· Heat the Santorini fava, add some liquid if needed and dress. Griddle the vegetables and place on the table.
· Make the Orecchiette pasta and the brown butter and set aside to dress when your guests arrive.
· Finish the minestrone and keep warm.

*When your guests arrive:*
· Serve them a drink, place the falafel in the oven to heat and serve with the grapefruit & sumac yogurt.

*Whilst your guests are helping themselves to fava and falafel:*
· Finish the pasta and bring to the table with the Simple butternut & greens.
· Then serve the minestrone with chilli oil.
· Clear the decks and bring out the Chocolate mud cake with whisky & blood orange cream.

*Maximize flavour*

This recipe uses fresh chillies/chiles, which means that the shelf life is not as long as other chilli/chile oils, but I find the flavour cleaner.

## Fresh chilli oil

**250 ml/1 cup extra virgin olive oil**
**2–3 bird's eye chillies/chiles**
**a pinch of dried chilli/red pepper flakes**

*sterilized glass bottle (see page 4)*

MAKES 250 ML/1 CUP

Gently warm the olive oil in a saucepan. Add the chilli/red pepper flakes and whole chillies/chiles to the oil and heat for 3–4 minutes. Remove from the heat and leave the oil to cool slightly. Once cool, pour into a sterilized glass bottle.

The oil can be kept in the refrigerator for up to 2 weeks.

## Blood orange & rosemary negronis

When blood oranges are in season make the most of them and use them in this negroni. If you prefer to use normal oranges, they also work really well. This is not sweet but has a clean and light sour taste, a flavour that is great with savoury dishes.

**150 ml/⅔ cup Campari**
**150 ml/⅔ cup sweet (rosso) vermouth**
**100 ml/scant ½ cup gin**
**3–4 blood oranges, cut into wedges**
**8 sprigs of rosemary**
**ice cubes**

Half-fill a large jug/pitcher with ice cubes. Add the Campari, vermouth and gin and stir to combine. Refrigerate until ready to serve. Add more ice and garnish with blood orange wedges and rosemary sprigs just before serving.

## Crispy blood oranges

**1–2 blood oranges**
**1 tablespoon caster/granulated sugar**

*baking sheet lined with parchment paper*

Preheat the oven to 70°C (160°F) or the lowest gas setting. Thinly slice the oranges (with the peel on), place on the baking sheet and sprinkle with sugar. Place in the oven, keep the oven door slightly ajar and dehydrate them in the oven until crispy and dry – this usually takes a few hours.

### Make it pretty

Using edible decorations such as blood orange crisps makes a dish beautiful and delicious at the same time – I like to serve these with the chocolate cake on page 67. You can use this method for all types of citrus.

# Santorini fava with griddled radicchio & little gem lettuce wedges

This recipe is a great all-rounder. I first ate it in Santorini where it is served as part of a mezze, but then discovered that it is eaten all over Greece as a humble meal. You can make a batch of this and serve it as a dip and then later in the week as a mid-week meal. It absorbs a lot of moisture, so add some liquid if reheating it. I like to finish it with lots of herbs, a dollop of yogurt and a good glug of chilli oil (see page 58).

3 little gem lettuce, halved
2 radicchio, halved
2 tablespoons olive oil
½ red onion, thinly sliced, to serve
2 tablespoons capers, drained, to serve
sea salt and freshly ground black pepper
crusty bread, to serve

SANTORINI FAVA
250 g/2¼ cups yellow split peas
3 tablespoons olive oil (1 tablespoon reserved for finishing)
1 red onion, roughly chopped
2 cloves of garlic, crushed
5 sprigs of thyme, leaves picked
3 sprigs of oregano, leaves picked
1 teaspoon tomato paste or sundried tomato paste
2 bay leaves
600 ml/2½ cups warm vegetable stock
juice of 1 lemon
½ teaspoon paprika
a pinch of chilli/red pepper flakes
sea salt and freshly ground black pepper

SERVES 6

To make the fava, rinse the split peas in plenty of water. Heat a large saucepan over a medium-high heat, add 2 tablespoons of the olive oil, the chopped onion, garlic, thyme and oregano and sauté.

As soon as the onions start to caramelize, add the tomato paste and cook for 5 minutes, then add the split peas and bay leaves and stir. Pour in the warm stock, turn the heat down to medium and season well with salt and pepper. Simmer with the lid on for 40–50 minutes until the split peas are thick and mushy. While the split peas are boiling, white foam will probably surface on the water – remove this with a slotted spoon.

Meanwhile, for the griddled vegetables, heat up a griddle/grill pan and lightly brush with olive oil. Season the lettuce and radicchio with salt and pepper and griddle on each side until slightly charred and soft but still with bite.

Pour the lemon juice into the pan of split peas, add the paprika and chilli/red pepper flakes and transfer the mixture into a food processor, or alternatively, if you prefer a coarser texture, don't process. Mix until the peas become smooth and creamy, like a purée.

Serve the fava with the remaining olive oil drizzled over, and with the griddled vegetables, sliced onions, capers and crusty bread.

# Simple butternut & greens

This salad is one you can add to, to make it into a meal — bacon and blue cheese or cooked quinoa all work well.

1 small butternut
  squash, roasted
  (approx. 600 g/21 oz.)
50 g/2 cups rocket/
  arugula
100 g/2 cups tenderstem
  broccoli, steamed
50 g/2 cups baby spinach
50 ml/3½ tablespoons
  vinaigrette (see
  page 49)

10 g/¼ cup chives,
  roughly chopped
30 g/1 oz. pomegranate
  seeds
50 g/2 oz. feta cheese,
  crumbled
10 g/1 tablespoon
  pumpkin seeds,
  lightly toasted

SERVES 6

In a bowl mix the squash, rocket/arugula, broccoli, spinach, vinaigrette, chives, pomegranate seeds and feta cheese and sprinkle with pumpkin seeds.

# Orecchiette with brussels sprouts & burnt butter

Make sure you allow the butter to cook until almost brown in colour and with a nutty scent and flavour.

200 g/7 oz. Brussels
  sprouts, trimmed and
  halved
2 tablespoons olive oil
4 sprigs of thyme
2 garlic cloves, peeled
  and crushed
350 g/12 oz. dried
  orecchiette pasta
100 g/1 stick minus
  1 tablespoon unsalted
  butter, diced

a handful of freshly
  chopped parsley,
  mint and basil,
  roughly chopped
juice of ½ lemon
150 g/5 oz. chopped
  hazelnuts, toasted
3 tablespoons grated
  Parmesan
sea salt and freshly
  ground black pepper

SERVES 6

Preheat the oven to 180°C (350°F) Gas 4.

Toss the sprouts with 1 tablespoon of the olive oil, the thyme and garlic and arrange cut-side down on a baking sheet. Sprinkle with salt and pepper. Roast in the preheated oven for 18–20 minutes or until the sprouts are tender, depending on the size of the sprouts.

Meanwhile, cook the pasta according to the package instructions. Drain, reserving a few tablespoons of the cooking water. Return the pasta to the pot.

Put the butter in a large frying pan/skillet and place over a medium heat. Cook for 4–5 minutes until melted and the butter has turned a deep nut-brown colour, swirling the pan often. Season to taste. Add the mixed herbs, lemon juice and toasted hazelnuts.

Add the sprouts, Parmesan, a few tablespoons of the reserved pasta water and the burnt butter mixture to the pasta. Mix and serve in a large bowl.

# Watercress falafel with grapefruit & sumac yogurt

These are cooked in the oven instead being fried, making them healthier. The watercress brings an earthier flavour, while grapefruit and sumac add a clean, fresh twist.

FALAFEL
- 2 cans chickpeas/ garbanzo beans, drained
- 1 tablespoon tahini
- 1 teaspoon salt
- 1 teaspoon baking powder
- 1 teaspoon cumin seeds
- ½ teaspoon chilli/red pepper flakes
- 1 garlic clove, crushed
- 100 g/2 cups watercress, roughly chopped, plus extra to serve
- ½ bunch of coriander/ cilantro, roughly chopped
- 2 tablespoons plain/ all-purpose flour
- juice of ½ lemon
- 3 tablespoons olive oil
- ½ grapefruit, peeled and segmented, to serve
- a handful of coriander/ cilantro, to serve

SUMAC YOGURT
- 100 g/½ cup thick Greek-style yogurt
- 50 g/¼ cup tahini paste
- 1 teaspoon sumac
- 1 tablespoon olive oil
- grated zest and juice of ½ grapefruit

SERVES 6 AS A SHARING DISH

Preheat the oven to 220°C (425°F) Gas 7.

To make the falafel, place the chickpeas/garbanzo beans in a food processor with the tahini, salt, baking powder, cumin, chilli/red pepper flakes, garlic, watercress, coriander/ cilantro, flour and lemon juice. Whizz until very finely chopped but not puréed. Place a large roasting pan in the oven to heat up. Using a wet hand, shape the mixture into 16 balls, then flatten slightly into patties.

Add the oil to the roasting pan, return to the oven for 2 minutes, then carefully add the falafel, tossing to coat them in hot oil. Bake for 25 minutes, turning once, until crisp and golden.

Meanwhile in a bowl mix the yogurt, tahini, sumac, olive oil and grapefruit zest and juice and set aside. Serve the falafel with segments of grapefruit, watercress and coriander/cilantro on a platter with the bowl of sumac yogurt.

# Winter root veg minestrone

This is one of those dishes that can be made in advance and finished with a few last additions of green vegetables before serving. It's hearty, healthy and a really affordable way of feeding a crowd. What really elevates it is the addition of Parmesan, fresh basil and the chilli/chile oil.

Preheat the oven to 200°C (400°F) Gas 6.

Toss the carrot, parsnip, new potatoes and fennel seeds in olive oil, season and tip onto the prepared baking sheet. Roast in the preheated oven for 30 minutes.

Add a splash of oil to a large heavy-based pot over a medium heat. Add the onion, garlic, celery and fennel and sweat, stirring frequently, for 15 minutes.

Add the bay leaves, thyme and tomato paste to the pot and cook for 2 minutes, stirring. Add the roasted vegetables, cannellini beans, stock and 1 litre/4¼ cups water and bring to a simmer. Add the green beans and kale and cook for 15 minutes. Add the pasta for the last 8 minutes of cooking.

Keep an eye on the level of the liquid. It should be a thick soup, but you may have to add a little more water.

Serve with shaved Parmesan, basil leaves and a drizzle of chilli/chile oil, and some crusty bread on the side, if you wish.

1 carrot, peeled and roughly chopped
1 parsnip, peeled and roughly chopped
50 g/2 oz. new potatoes, scrubbed and quartered
1 teaspoon fennel seeds
2 tablespoons extra virgin olive oil
1 brown onion, peeled and roughly chopped
3 garlic cloves, peeled and crushed
4 celery stalks, diced
1 bulb fennel, diced
2 fresh bay leaves
4 sprigs of thyme, leaves picked

3 tablespoons tomato paste
1 can cannellini beans, rinsed
800 ml/scant 3½ cups vegetable stock (a stock cube is fine)
100 g/3½ oz. green beans, cut into 4 cm/1½ in. lengths
50 g/2 oz. curly kale
2 handfuls of short pasta
shaved Parmesan, basil and Chilli oil (see page 58), to serve

*baking sheet lined with parchment paper*

SERVES 6

# Chocolate mud cake
## with whisky & blood orange cream

This is my favourite cake of all time. It's dense, deep, moist, decadent, rich but not very sweet. Serving it with the Whisky & blood orange cream makes it very grown up.

250 g/2¼ sticks unsalted butter, chopped
200 g/7 oz. dark/ bittersweet chocolate, chopped
250 ml/1 cup full-fat/ whole milk
80 ml/⅓ cup whisky or brandy
330 g/1½ cups plus 2 tablespoons caster/ granulated sugar
1 teaspoon vanilla extract
1 teaspoon instant coffee
3 eggs
200 g/1½ cups plain/ all-purpose flour, sifted
60 g/2 oz. self-raising/ rising flour, sifted
25 g/2 tablespoons cocoa powder, sifted, plus extra for dusting
Crispy blood oranges (see page 59), to serve

CHOCOLATE GANACHE ICING
150 g/5 oz. dark/ bittersweet chocolate, chopped
1–2 teaspoons golden/ light corn syrup, or to taste
125 ml/½ cup double/ heavy cream

WHISKY & BLOOD ORANGE CREAM
200 ml/scant 1 cup double/heavy cream
20 ml/4 teaspoons whisky or brandy
juice of 1 blood orange
2–3 tablespoons caster/ superfine sugar, or to taste

*28 x 20 cm/11 x 8 in. baking pan, lightly greased*

SERVES 10

Preheat the oven to 150°C (300°F) Gas 2.

Place the butter, chocolate, milk, whisky, sugar, vanilla and coffee in a large saucepan over a medium heat and stir occasionally for 6 minutes or until melted and smooth. Set aside to cool slightly. Add the eggs and whisk to combine. Pour into a large bowl, add the flours and cocoa and whisk until smooth.

Pour into the prepared baking pan and bake in the preheated oven for 40 minutes or until cooked when tested with a skewer. Allow to cool completely in the baking pan, then remove.

To make the chocolate ganache icing, heat the chocolate, syrup and cream in a small saucepan over a low heat, stirring, until melted and smooth. Set aside to cool completely.

Meanwhile, for the blood orange cream, whisk the cream, whisky, blood orange juice and sugar until light and fluffy and set aside.

When the cake has cooled, spread the chocolate ganache icing over the top and allow to set. Either top with the blood orange cream or serve it on the side, along with the crispy blood oranges.

# Simple sharing

Entertaining need not be difficult – it should be fun, relaxed and warm for you and your guests. This menu is effortless and very casual, and perfect for a games afternoon or just a simple fuss-free gathering with those you love. Simple and tasty – what more could you want?

## Menu

Margaritas with jalapeños

Spicy sweet potato wedges & corn
with harissa crème fraîche

Scorched padrón peppers

Chorizo & three-bean smoky nacho
platter with avocado & coriander
smash & jalapeňo yogurt

Vietnamese bánh mì
filled baguettes

Asian slaw

Superfood caesar salad

Sundae station

## PARTY PLANNING

To get ahead and extend your chill time with your friends:

*The night before:*
· Slow cook the pulled pork. Allow to cool and refrigerate.
· In the morning: make the Chorizo & three bean sauce and the tortilla chips and set aside. Make the Superfood caesar salad dressing and chill until ready to use.

*One hour before:*
· Make the Spicy sweet potato wedges & corn with harissa crème fraîche.
· Prepare all the ingredients for the bánh mì, make the Superfood caesar salad (reserve the dressing for later).
· Make the Avocado & coriander smash and build the nacho platter, top with cheese.
· Gently heat the pulled pork for the Vietnamese bánh mì filled baguettes.

*When your friends arrive:*
· Blitz the margaritas and prep the glasses or better still delegate the task!
· Make the Scorched padrón peppers and serve them with the margaritas.
· Once the pulled pork is heated through, make the bánh mì and serve on a platter or board.
· Grill the nachos and take to the table. Dress the Superfood caesar salad and take to the table.
· Share the food and have fun.
· For the Sundae station, place all the sauces, toppings and ice creams on a board or platter and let everyone dig in!
· Make sure that you get your friends to help you clean up before they leave!

## Margaritas with jalapeños

This classic drink is definitely great for a crowd! Refreshing with a touch of heat from the addition of the jalapeño pepper.

**300 ml/1¼ cups tequila**
**juice from 6 limes, plus 2 limes**
   **cut into wedges, to serve**
**3 tablespoons agave syrup**
**5 cups ice cubes**
**3 tablespoons fine sea salt**
**1 jalapeño, sliced**

SERVES 6

Put the tequila, lime juice, agave syrup and ice in a blender and blend until smooth. Pour the salt onto a plate and moisten the rims of 6 glasses with a lime wedge. Dip the rim of each glass into the salt and pour in the margaritas. Serve with lime wedges and a slice of jalapeño in each glass.

## Spicy sweet potato wedges & corn with harissa crème fraîche

These spicy potato wedges and corn have a great kick to them. A perfect side and vegetarian alternative.

1 tablespoon ground coriander
1 tablespoon ground cumin
1 tablespoon smoked paprika
½ teaspoon chilli/chili powder
2 garlic cloves, crushed
3 tablespoons olive oil
3 sweet potatoes, scrubbed
   and cut into wedges
220 g/8 oz. baby corn
sea salt and freshly ground
   black pepper

HARISSA CRÈME FRAÎCHE
1–2 tablespoons harissa paste
100 g/½ cup crème fraîche

*large baking dish lined with parchment paper*

SERVES 6 AS A SIDE

Preheat the oven to 200°C (400°F) Gas 6. Put the spices and the garlic in a large bowl. Add the oil and potato wedges and mix well. Arrange the wedges in a single layer in the baking dish. Sprinkle generously with sea salt. Bake in the oven for 45 minutes until tender and crisp. Add the corn and cook for a further 10 minutes. Transfer to a serving bowl. Swirl the harissa through the crème fraîche. Serve alongside the wedges.

## Scorched padrón peppers

Another classic but perfect accompaniment to the margarita! Very simple yet light and full of flavour.

1–2 tablespoons olive oil
120 g/4½ oz. padrón peppers
black salt or pink Himalayan salt

SERVES 6 AS AN APPETIZER

Heat a frying pan/skillet over a high heat and add the olive oil. When the oil is hot and shimmering, add the peppers. Cook and stir the peppers until the skin is brown and blistered.

Remove the peppers from the pan, place on a plate and sprinkle with salt to taste. Serve immediately.

# Chorizo & three-bean smoky nacho platter with avocado & coriander smash & jalapeño yogurt

This is a twist on a Mexican classic and can be a great vegetarian option if you omit the chorizo and add an extra teaspoon of smoked paprika. The smoky bean mix can become the perfect topping to a bowl of rice the next day.

3 wholemeal/whole-wheat tortillas, cut into triangles or 100 g/3½ cups blue corn tortilla chips

oil, for spraying and frying

190 g/1½ cups chorizo, roughly chopped

1 red onion, roughly chopped

1 tablespoon ground cumin

1 large bunch of coriander/cilantro, stems finely chopped, leaves reserved

1 red chilli/chile, finely chopped

2 tablespoons tomato paste

1 tablespoon smoked chipotle paste

2 garlic cloves, crushed

1 teaspoon dried oregano

½ teaspoon smoked paprika

100 ml/⅓ cup vegetable stock

400 g/14 oz. can black beans

400 g/14 oz. can kidney beans

400 g/14 oz. can aduki beans

400 g/14 oz. can tomatoes

1 tablespoon Worcestershire sauce

TO SERVE

50 g/½ cup sliced olives

a handful of grated mozzarella

Jalapeño yogurt (see page 73)

Avocado & coriander smash (see page 73)

100 g/½ cup queso fresca or crumbled feta cheese

*two baking sheets lightly sprayed with oil*

SERVES 6

If using tortillas, preheat the oven to 200°C (400°F) Gas 6. Arrange the tortilla triangles in a single layer on the baking sheets. Lightly spray with oil. Bake for 5–6 minutes or until golden. Cool on a wire rack.

Heat the oil in a large frying pan/skillet over a medium heat. Add the chorizo and onion and cook, stirring, for 5 minutes or until the onion is soft. Increase the heat to high. Add the ground cumin, coriander/cilantro stems and chilli/chile and cook, stirring, for 1 minute. Add the tomato paste, chipotle paste, garlic, oregano and smoked paprika and stir for a further minute. Stir in the vegetable stock, beans, canned tomatoes and Worcestershire sauce, bring to the boil and gently boil for 10 minutes or until thickened. (Beans can be made the day before and kept in the fridge, reheat before using.)

To assemble, preheat the grill/broiler to medium/high and arrange the nachos on a large plate, top with the beans, olives and a handful of grated mozzarella. Place under the grill/broiler until the mozzarella has melted. Serve with queso fresca, the reserved coriander/cilantro leaves and crumbled queso fresca, and the Jalapeño yogurt and Avocado & coriander smash on the side.

This recipe deliberately makes a large quantity of the smoky beans as they are so good eaten as leftovers!

## Avocado & coriander smash

1 tablespoon coriander seeds
1 garlic clove
2 tablespoons olive oil
1 large bunch of coriander/
   cilantro
3 small avocados, or 2 large,
   peeled and stoned/pitted
juice of 1–2 limes (depending
   on sharpness)
sea salt and freshly ground
   black pepper

In a frying pan/skillet dry roast the coriander seeds until fragrant and allow to cool.

In a food processor place three-quarters of the seeds, the garlic, 1 tablespoon olive oil and the coriander/cilantro and blitz to a coarse paste. Roughly chop the avocado on a chopping board, add half the lime juice, a drizzle of olive oil and the salt and pepper and keep mashing with the knife to make a chunky, smashed mixture. Transfer to a serving bowl and swirl the paste through. Finish with the remaining oil, salt and pepper, lime juice and coriander seeds.

## Jalapeño yogurt

150 g/½ cup Greek yogurt
30 g/1 oz. pickled jalapeños, chopped
1 tablespoon olive oil
sea salt and freshly ground
   black pepper

In a bowl swirl the yogurt with the jalapeños, olive oil and salt and pepper.

# Vietnamese bánh mì filled baguettes

The baguette was introduced to Vietnam when the French colonized and today this recipe is the perfect East meets West dish! The deep flavours of the pulled pork with the crispiness of the slaw and fresh herbs are delicious. If your guests prefer to remain carb free, you could serve the filling in the cabbage or lettuce leaves. A cheat's way to make a bánh mì is to buy a cooked rôtisserie chicken, pull it apart and serve with the slaw and sauces.

1 onion, roughly diced
1.6 kg/3½ lb. skinless and off-the-bone pork shoulder
2 lemongrass stalks, bruised
2 garlic cloves, smashed
1 thumb-sized piece of ginger, thickly sliced
4 tablespoons char siu (Asian barbecue) sauce
3 tablespoons rice vinegar
½ tablespoon fish sauce
1 tablespoon soy sauce
2 tablespoons palm sugar
50 ml/3½ tablespoons vegetable stock

TO SERVE
2 baguettes
3 iceberg lettuce leaves
3 cabbage leaves
Asian slaw (see page 77)
Thai basil leaves
sriracha
Maggi seasoning (optional)

Sprinkle the onion over the base of a slow cooker and place the piece of pork on top. If the pork is too large for your cooker it can be cut in half. Add the lemongrass.

In a jug/pitcher, combine the garlic, ginger, char siu sauce, vinegar, fish sauce, soy sauce and palm sugar, stir to combine, pour over the pork and cover the slow cooker.

Turn the slow cooker on to low and cook for 8 hours. When cooked, the pork should just fall apart. Place onto a large tray that will collect the juices and gently tease and pull the meat apart with your fingers or 2 forks. Before returning the pork to the juices, skim any excess fat. Return the pork to the slow cooker and toss through the pan juices. Cover and keep warm.

To serve, split the baguettes in half (or open out the lettuce or cabbage leaves). Fill with the pulled pork, Asian slaw and basil leaves, and top with extra seasoning if you wish.

VARIATION
If you don't have a slow cooker, preheat the oven to 110°C (225°F) Gas ¼. Place the pork in a large baking dish and cover tightly with foil. Bake in the preheated oven for 8 hours. Extra pulled pork can be frozen in its juices for up 3 months.

# Asian slaw

¼ Asian cabbage, thinly
sliced
2 small carrots, shredded
2 spring onions/
scallions, thinly sliced
on the diagonal
a handful of coriander/
cilantro
a handful of Thai basil
crispy fried shallots, to
serve (optional)

DRESSING
2 tablespoons rice
vinegar
2 tablespoons sweet
chilli/chili sauce
1 tablespoon fish sauce

SERVES 6

Place the cabbage, carrots, spring onions/scallions,
herbs and shallots in a large mixing bowl and toss
together. Mix together the ingredients for the
dressing and toss the dressing through the slaw
ingredients just before serving.

# Superfood caesar salad

Just a touch healthier and definitely a twist
on the original, this is a perfect base for
some shredded chicken or sliced boiled
eggs. As part of this feast I have kept it
simple, but as a main meal, the addition
of protein would make it more substantial.

2 slices of rye
sourdough bread
1 tablespoon olive oil
½ celeriac, peeled and
grated
a handful of kale
3 Cos lettuce leaves,
cut in large pieces
2 beetroot/beets, peeled
and grated
20 g/¾ oz. shaved
Parmesan
shredded poached
chicken (optional)
7-minute boiled/cooked
eggs (optional)

BASIL CAESAR
DRESSING
2 eggs
1 garlic clove, crushed
juice of 1 lemon
2 teaspoons Dijon
mustard
a dash of
Worcestershire sauce
3 anchovies in olive oil
a handful of basil
200 ml/scant 1 cup olive
oil
sea salt and freshly
ground black pepper

baking sheet lined with
parchment paper

SERVES 6

To make the dressing, whizz together the eggs,
garlic, lemon juice, Dijon mustard, Worcestershire
sauce, 2 anchovies and the basil in a small food
processor. Season well with sea salt and black
pepper, then keep the food processor running and
gradually pour in the olive oil until the dressing
becomes really thick and glossy. Set aside.

Preheat the oven to 200°C (400°F) Gas 6.

To make the croutons, chop the slices of rye
bread into rough cubes. Toss the croutons with
the olive oil in a bowl and season with salt and
pepper. Spread the cubes out in one layer on the
prepared baking sheet and bake in the preheated
oven for 10–15 minutes until toasted. Set aside
to cool.

Assembly can be done last minute, but prepare
the celeriac in advance by storing it in some water
with a squeeze of lemon juice in it to stop the
celeriac from discolouring.

To serve, lay the kale, lettuce leaves, beetroot/
beets, celeriac, croutons and Parmesan shavings
on a platter, then drizzle over the dressing. Top
with shredded chicken or sliced eggs, if using.

# Sundae station

So yes, this is naughty and yes, it's a cheat's way to finish your party. Be creative and let people make their own – it really brings people together to share.

**1 tub strawberry ice cream**
**1 tub chocolate ice cream**
**1 tub vanilla ice cream**

TOPPINGS
**ready-made jelly/jello**
**ready-made chocolate sauce**
**ready-made caramel sauce**
**wafers**
**pretzels**
**mini marshmallows**
**berry sauce (see page 157)**
**selection of brownies
  and cookies**

Serve the tubs of ice cream on a tray with bowls and jars of toppings, where people can create their own sundaes. Make them fun for adults by pouring some Irish cream or coffee (or both) over the caramel and pretzel sundae.

*Make it pretty*

Scatter plenty of cushions on the floor around your coffee table, push back the furniture and let everyone spread out and lounge around for a thoroughly relaxed gathering.

A special dinner or an easy supper, but always
impressive! The key to throwing a memorable
dinner party, while also being able to escape
from the kitchen while it's all happening,
is putting a little thought into your menu.

# DINNER

# Craft beer & cheese night

A really chilled way to get together with friends and share wonderful craft beers with autumnal food.

## PARTY PLANNING

A lot of this menu can be made in advance.

*A few or more days before:*
· Make the Quince in ale and honey and refrigerate; make the pickles and refrigerate; make the soda bread and freeze.

*The day before:*
· Make the chicken pie filling and refrigerate.
· Buy the cheese and beer and chill.

*On the morning:*
· Top the pie with the potatoes and chill.
· Defrost the bread.
· Make the Individual apple pies and set aside.

*One hour before your guests arrive:*
· Place the cheese on a board to allow to come to room temperature. Glaze the apple pies. Gently heat the bread and place with the cheese board, bring out the quince and pickles. Make the slaw but set aside the dressing for service.

*When your guests arrive:*
· Serve them a beer and lead them to the cheese board. Yes, it's controversial to serve it before the meal and with beer! But go on, live a little.
· Place the pie in the oven and when it's ready, serve it with the slaw.

*For the finale:*
· Serve the pies either ever so slightly heated (not too much) or at room temperature, which is my favourite way. Don't forget the drizzle of cream.

*Maximize flavour*

Keep the cooking juices from the quince; these will be a syrupy amber nectar and perfect drizzled over cheese and bread.

# Craft brewing industry

With all the choices that are now available, choosing beer can be a bit overwhelming, particularly if you are new to the craft beer scene. There are no hard and fast rules about how to select beers, but these guidelines have been provided by friend and beer expert, Catherine LeBlanc.

To narrow the field, you may wish to start with local breweries and see what options and styles are available and branch out from there. For a dinner party, you will probably want to keep the alcohol by volume (ABV) under 6%. If you would like to serve a lager, pale ale or India pale ale (IPA), check to see if there is a brewed-on or best-by date – the fresher the better. Otherwise, most beer keeps quite well when kept away from direct sunlight and within a normal temperature range. Remember when choosing your beers that good craft beer is available in both bottles and cans – do not assume that beer in a can is only for impoverished university students! Some of the most interesting and innovative craft brewers can their beer.

A speciality beer shop (in your area if possible) is likely to have the widest selection of properly stored beers as well as knowledgeable staff – and they may have samples! Just as you would seek the advice of a sommelier to choose wine for a dinner party, ask for advice when trying to navigate the variety of styles and flavours of beers. If a dedicated beer store is not accessible to you, many wine shops, grocery stores and corner stores now carry craft beer. If you find yourself unable to choose, ask other customers if they have favourites. As a general rule, people who are interested in craft beer tend to be friendly and excited to share what knowledge they have.

# Cheese & beer – pairing & tasting notes

## Goat cheese & a saison

Try pairing soft goat's cheese with saison-style beer. Saisons were traditionally brewed by Belgian farmers during the winter, stored through the spring and consumed throughout the summer. They tend to be on the drier side, with a light fruitiness and sweet yeastiness balanced by a mild bitter herbal quality. The fruity quality of the beer's yeast complements the tang of goat's cheese, while the light malt and body of the beer balance out the creaminess of the cheese. Both the beer and the cheese will be light, working together to bring out the subtle flavours and textures in each. Choose a log or wheel of soft cheese, with or without ash, looking for something that is more soft and crumbly rather than gooey at the centre.

## Farmhouse Cheddar & an English pale ale

This is a classic combination. English-style pale ales tend to be maltier and less bitter than American-style pale ales, with a medium body and colouring that ranges from deep gold to copper. This malty character brings an almost sweet, bready flavour that goes perfectly with rich, salty Cheddar. The mild bitterness from the hops also complements the nutty, earthiness of the cheese. Farmhouse Cheddars come in giant wheels so the cheesemonger will cut you a wedge. Most tend to be pale to golden, but some can be orange. The texture may be a bit drier compared to vacuum-packed Cheddar, and you may spot a blue vein or two in sections of the wheel, but this is normal for traditional Cheddars and what you will want.

## Storage & serving

To store your cheeses, wrap each in waxed paper and keep in the refrigerator. Remove a few hours before serving to allow the still-wrapped cheeses to come to room temperature to enjoy the optimum texture and flavours.

To serve, unwrap the cheese and place on a serving board with a separate cheese knife for each, and a varied selection of accompaniments – such as plain crackers or toasted baguette points, plum chutney, fruit jam/jelly or paste and honeycomb.

To store your beers, keep in a dark, cool place. At least a few hours in advance of serving, put them in the refrigerator to cool. Remove the beers 10–15 minutes before you are ready to serve them to allow some of the flavours to be released as they come to temperature.

A general rule of thumb is to serve and consume beers from light to dark, leaving the beers with the strongest flavours for last to avoid compromising your palate. In this case, the order would be: saison, sour, bitter, stout. Some people recommend that specific beers should be served in speciality glassware to encourage aromas to be enjoyed more easily, to regulate the flow of each sip, and to retain the frothy head. Do not worry about this for your party – it is important, however, to use clean glassware for each beer. Tilt the glass when pouring, turning upright when you have poured about three-quarters of the liquid. For the last one-quarter, pour slowly into the upright glass to allow for a bit of foamy head to remain.

As with wine, sniffing a beer before tasting is key to enjoying it. You may be surprised by some of the aromas you detect, and how they compare with the taste of the beer.

## Washed rind soft cheese & a sour

If you are feeling adventurous, try pairing a bold, washed rind cheese with a sour-style beer (such as a classic lambic or geuze). Historically these beers were created through spontaneous fermentation after exposure to wild yeasts, taking years to mature and giving them tart, funky characteristics. They tend to be light in body and often fruit is added to encourage second fermentation, resulting in subtle fruit flavours and aromas alongside the crisp, tart acidity from the wild yeasts. The same bold and earthy flavours found in these beers appear in washed rind cheeses and when paired together, are intensified. The acidity and carbonation of the beer help cut the creaminess of the cheese and cleanse the palate to create a strong but well-balanced match. Look for a cheese round with a textured rind and a soft, slightly gooey centre. Often the more intensely flavoured cheeses have orange or gold rind.

## Blue & a stout

Many of the principles that make Stilton and port a great combination hold true for pairing blue cheese and stout. Stouts are deep brown to black, with a heavy body and smooth feel. Many have the aroma and taste of chocolate or coffee due to the roasting of the malt but some are brewed with these ingredients to intensify the flavours. The smooth body of a stout complements the rich creaminess of blue cheese. At the same time, the deeply roasted malt creates the chocolate and fruity sweetness of a stout – the same flavours that can go unnoticed in an earthy blue cheese. Look for cheese that is buttery, creamy or crumbly with subtle blue vein lacing. These cheeses have both sweet and nutty characteristics along with salty and earthy flavours that pair nicely with a stout.

# Fruit & nut spice soda bread

This is a great, quick, no-knead, no-prove bread which works well with everything, so make several at a time and freeze them. I absolutely love this bread with cheese! This pairs well with a saison.

70 g/½ cup mixed dried fruit, such as dates and (dark) raisins
1 tablespoon maple syrup
400 g/3 cups plain/all-purpose flour or wholemeal/whole-wheat flour
100 g/1 cup oats, plus extra to finish
1 teaspoon mixed/apple pie spice
a pinch of sea salt
50 g/3½ tablespoons butter
1 teaspoon bicarbonate of soda/baking soda
50 g/½ cup walnuts, toasted and roughly chopped
350 ml/1½ cups buttermilk

*baking sheet lined with parchment paper*

SERVES 6

Preheat the oven to 200°C (400°F) Gas 6.

Place the fruit in a small bowl and just cover with boiling water. Stir in the maple syrup and leave to infuse.

Mix the flour, oats, mixed/apple pie spice and salt in a large bowl. Rub in the butter until the mixture resembles coarse breadcrumbs. Stir in the bicarbonate of soda/baking soda, strain the fruit, discarding the liquid and add to the flour mix. Stir in the nuts.

Add the buttermilk and mix very gently until you can bring the mix together into a soft but not sticky dough. Tip out onto the prepared baking sheet and form into a slightly rounded loaf 4.5 cm/1¾ in. tall and top with the extra oats.

Flour a wooden spoon handle and use it to press in a cross about 2 cm/¾ in. deep on the top of the loaf. Bake in the preheated oven for 35–45 minutes for a large loaf, until it is well risen and golden. At this stage turn it over, lower the temperature to 170°C (350°F) Gas 4 and cook it for an extra 5–10 minutes. Cool on a rack covered with a clean kitchen towel. This is best eaten the same day or allow to cool and freeze.

# Quince in ale & honey

This is another one of those dishes that goes well with savoury food such as cheese board. This pairs well with a saison or stout.

3 quinces, scrubbed
150 g/¾ cup light brown sugar
100 g/5½ tablespoons runny honey
grated zest and juice of 1 lemon
grated zest and juice of 1 orange
1 teaspoon vanilla paste
350 ml/1½ cups pale ale
1 cinnamon stick
4 cloves
3 cardamom pods, bruised
5 fresh bay leaves
2 tablespoons maple syrup

SERVES 6

Preheat the oven to 140°C (275°F) Gas 1.

Cut the quinces into quarters and lay them in a ceramic baking dish, cut-side up. Scatter over the sugar, drizzle with the honey, add the lemon and orange zest and juice and pour over the ale. Add the cinnamon, cloves, cardamom and bay leaves, cover with parchment paper and foil and bake in the preheated oven for 2 hours.

Uncover and add the maple syrup, then cook for a further 2 hours. You can serve the quince hot or at room temperature, although once refrigerated they will need to be warmed through.

# Bread & butter pickles

When it comes to making this pickle, I don't follow the rules! These are great eaten with the cheese board, with your favourite barbecued meat, on a burger or to finish a cream cheese-topped cracker. This pairs well with a saison or stout.

400 g/14 oz. small Lebanese cucumbers, sliced
1 tablespoon sea salt
1 onion, thinly sliced
180 g/1 cup granulated sugar
250 ml/1 cup white vinegar
100 ml/⅓ cup apple cider vinegar
50 g/¼ cup light brown sugar
1½ teaspoons yellow mustard seeds
1 teaspoon celery seeds
a pinch of ground turmeric

MAKES 1 LARGE JAR

In a bowl combine the sliced cucumbers and salt, cover and chill for 1½ hours. Transfer the cucumber into a colander and rinse thoroughly under cold water. Drain well, and return the cucumber to the bowl. Add the onion to the bowl and toss with the cucumber.

Combine the granulated sugar, white vinegar, apple cider vinegar, brown sugar, mustard seeds, celery seeds and ground turmeric in a saucepan; bring to a simmer over a medium heat, stirring until the sugar dissolves. Pour the hot vinegar mixture over the cucumber mixture; let stand at room temperature for 1 hour. Store in an airtight container in the refrigerator for up to 2 weeks.

# Chicken pie topped with potato & thyme crust

This is the perfect non-pastry pie, and great for gluten-free guests. The pie mixture is very versatile and you can make it in advance. As a variation, you could replace the potato topping with shop-bought puff pastry. This dish pairs well with an English pale ale.

20 g/4 teaspoons butter
1 tablespoon flavourless oil
2 leeks, cleaned and thinly sliced
1 carrot, finely chopped
2 celery stalks, finely chopped
3 garlic cloves, crushed
4 sprigs of thyme, leaves picked and chopped
700 g/1½ lb. skinless chicken thighs, cut into chunks
2 tablespoons plain/all-purpose flour (gluten-free if necessary)
200 ml/scant 1 cup white wine
200 ml/scant 1 cup chicken stock
1 bay leaf
1 teaspoon wholegrain mustard
1 teaspoon Dijon mustard
2 tablespoons double/heavy cream
freshly grated nutmeg
sea salt

TOPPING
1 kg/2 lb. 3 oz. small Desirée potatoes, thinly sliced
30 g/2 tablespoons butter, melted
8 sprigs of thyme, leaves picked
sea salt and freshly ground black pepper

SERVES 6

Heat the butter and oil in a heavy-based pan, add the leeks, carrot, celery, garlic and thyme and cook for 2 minutes until starting to soften. Add the chicken and cook gently without colouring for up to 10 minutes. Stir in the flour and cook for 1 minute. Pour in the wine and stir continuously, making sure that the wine reduces and the sauce thickens. Pour in the chicken stock one-third at a time, stirring continuously and making sure the sauce is thick and smooth before adding the next batch. Add the bay leaf, cover the pan and cook gently for 1 hour. Stir in the mustards, cream and freshly grated nutmeg to taste. Add salt if needed.

Preheat the oven to 180°C (350°F) Gas 4.

Meanwhile, bring a large pot of water to the boil, add the thinly sliced potatoes and boil for 12 minutes, take off the heat and drain well. Spread them out in a layer to allow the excess water to evaporate off.

Place the chicken mixture into a pie dish 24 cm/9½ in. in diameter and carefully lay the potatoes on top of the filling, overlapping them slightly, like a pie top.

Brush the potatoes with a little melted butter, season with salt and pepper and top with the thyme. Cook in the preheated oven for about 50 minutes. The pie is ready once the potatoes are cooked and golden brown.

# Rainbow slaw

This is crispy, crunchy and vibrant, and adds a freshness to the other earthy, autumnal dishes in this menu. It's the perfect side dish to serve with the chicken pie.

¼ white cabbage, finely shredded
½ purple cabbage, finely shredded
100 g/1 cup Brussels sprouts, thinly sliced
1 carrot, grated
1 small red onion, thinly sliced
2 tablespoons pumpkin seeds, toasted

DRESSING
100 ml/⅓ cup extra virgin olive oil
juice of 1 lemon
1 tablespoon apple cider vinegar
1 teaspoon runny honey
1 teaspoon Dijon mustard
a small bunch of parsley, finely chopped
½ small bunch of chives, finely chopped
2 sprigs of tarragon, finely chopped
sea salt and freshly ground black pepper

SERVES 6 AS A SIDE

In the serving dish place the dressing ingredients with the herbs and give it a good stir. Add all the other ingredients to the serving dish, season with salt and pepper and toss to combine. Serve immediately.

# Individual apple pies

This is a classic, super simple way to make an elegant tart. Change the fruit with the seasons. My all-time favourite is apple and drizzled with cream.

1 ready-made puff pastry sheet
3 Granny Smith apples
juice of ½ lemon
1 tablespoon brown sugar
1 teaspoon ground cinnamon
10 g/2 teaspoons unsalted butter
3 tablespoons apricot jam/jelly

*baking sheet lined with parchment paper*

MAKES 8

Preheat the oven to 180°C (350°F) Gas 4.

Roll the chilled dough out and cut into 8 equal rectangles. Using a fork, prick the pastry every 1 cm/½-in. to prevent air pockets from forming while it bakes. Place on the prepared baking sheet and refrigerate while you prepare the apples.

Cut the apples in half through the stem. Remove the stems and core them. Slice the apples crosswise into 1 cm/½ in. thick slices. Drizzle the lemon juice over the apples to prevent browning.

Place overlapping slices of the apples on the pastry rectangles, with 8–9 slices each. To keep things pretty, it's best not to use the smaller slices from the ends of the apples. Scatter sugar and cinnamon over the apples and dot with butter. Bake in the preheated oven for 20–25 minutes. Once the pastries are removed from the oven, put the apricot jam/jelly in a microwave-safe bowl and heat for 30 seconds. Brush on the pastries and serve with cream or ice cream.

# Fish fest

Fish is best when fresh and cooked just before you serve it –
I like to buy from a fishmonger and cook it that same day.
The less time between when it was swimming in the sea and
when you eat it the better! In fact, it should still smell like the
sea. With this menu, you can make most elements in advance
and cook the seafood just before you serve it.

## Menu

Lime, cucumber & lychee gin & tonic

Taramasalata, flat breads & pickled carrots
dipped in dukkah

Griddled shrimp & baby leek skewers
with tamari lime glaze

Baked salmon chops with vegetables

Pan-fried calamari with smoky chilli
& lemon salt

Wakame, pear & daikon salad

Frozen yogurt cake

*A few days before:*
- Make the Frozen yogurt cake and keep frozen.
- Make the Dukkah and store.

*On the day:*
- Make the Taramasalata and Pickled carrots.
- Marinate the shrimp and place on skewers with the leeks or spring onions/scallions.
- Marinate the salmon chops.

*One hour before:*
- Make the Wakame, pear & daikon salad, cover and set aside.
- Put together the Taramasalata platter, cover and set aside.
- Cook the new potatoes and place all the vegetables for the Baked salmon chops with vegetables in the baking dish and set aside, ready for the salmon.

*When your guests arrive:*
- Give them a hug, hand them a drink and lead them to the Taramasalata platter.
- Wait 20 minutes and then start cooking the prepared Griddled shrimp & baby leek skewers with tamari lime glaze and the Pan-fried calamari with smoky chilli and lemon salt and serve at the table – top up the drinks and dig in.
- After you have enjoyed your shrimp and calamari, finish off the salmon and cook.
- Once ready, serve with a green salad and make sure you drizzle those sauces.
- Bring the Frozen yogurt cake out and allow to sit for 20 minutes – serve with fresh fruit.

## Taramasalata, flat breads & pickled carrots dipped in dukkah

Making taramasalata from scratch is so worth it, and the smoky roe and lemon counterbalance each other perfectly. Taramasalata served alongside pickled carrots dipped in nutty dukkah is a good start to the meal.

**1 recipe Taramasalata (see page 98)**
**1 recipe Pickled carrots (see page 98)**
**100 g/3½ oz. pickled anchovies**
**12 crispy crackers or cream crackers**
**1 small pumpernickel loaf, sliced (optional)**
**100 g/3½ oz. salmon eggs**
**1 small bowl Dukkah (see page 98)**

SERVES 6

Arrange all the ingredients on a platter. Sprinkle a little of the dukkah over the carrots. Serve and share.

*Maximize flavour*

Keep flavoured salts in your store cupboard and use to jazz up any meal.

## Lime, cucumber & lychee gin & tonic

The combination of lime, cucumber and lychee is just magical – light, fresh, floral and with a gentle sweetness. A perfect pre-dinner drink.

**200 ml/scant 1 cup lychee juice**
**200 ml/scant 1 cup gin**
**½ cucumber, cut into thick slices**
**1 can lychees in syrup, drained**
**3 sprigs of mint, leaves picked**
**2 limes, sliced**
**ice cubes**

*cocktail sticks/toothpicks*

SERVES 6

Mix the lychee juice and gin in a jug/pitcher and add some ice. Take the cocktail sticks/toothpicks and thread on a piece of cucumber and a lychee and set aside.

Place some ice into the glasses, pour over the gin mixture, garnish with lime slices and mint leaves and top with a lychee and cucumber cocktail stick/toothpick.

## Make it pretty

To me, food is a feast for all the senses, so serving a pretty drink with a cute garnish that you can eat always works well. Pretty does not need to mean perfect! Not every drink needs to look the same. But make it tasty – taste above all means the most.

## Dukkah

A twist on the Egyptian classic. Perfect with bread or fresh vegetables.

100 g/¾ cup hazelnuts, skins removed
100 g/¾ cup almonds, skins removed
2 teaspoons fennel seeds
2 teaspoons cumin seeds
4 tablespoons coriander seeds
1 teaspoon sea salt
1 teaspoon pink peppercorns
3 tablespoons sesame seeds
1 tablespoon nigella seeds

*sterilized airtight container (see page 4)*

SERVES 6

Heat a frying pan/skillet. Add the nuts and lightly toast, then set aside. Add the fennel, cumin and coriander seeds to the pan and gently toast until aromatic. Once the seeds are golden, put them in a food processor with the sea salt and pink peppercorns and blitz very lightly. The mixture should be coarse. Lightly toast the sesame and nigella seeds and stir through the mixture.

The dukkah can be stored in an airtight container or jar for up to 6 weeks.

## Taramasalata

There are many ways to make taramasalata, but the most traditional – and best – method is with mashed potato and raw onion.

1 potato (approx. 200 g/7 oz.), peeled and chopped
1 red onion
150 g/5¼ oz. smoked codfish roe
juice of 2 lemons
3 tablespoons olive oil
salmon roe and lemon wedges, to serve (optional)

SERVES 6

Place the potato in a saucepan and cover with water. Bring to the boil, then reduce the heat and simmer until cooked through. Drain and set aside to cool a bit.

In a food processor blitz the onion into a purée, then add the roe, potato and lemon juice. Gradually add in the oil until thoroughly combined.

Transfer to a serving bowl. Chill until required.

## Pickled carrots

These are perfect served with a bowl of Dukkah.

12 mini heirloom carrots, leaves removed but leaving a small stalk (alternatively, use 3 large carrots quartered lengthways)
200 ml/scant 1 cup cider vinegar
100 g/½ cup coconut sugar
½ tablespoon coriander seeds
½ tablespoon mustard seeds
2 garlic cloves
2 tablespoons sea salt

*sterilized airtight container (see page 4)*

SERVES 6

Prepare the carrots and set aside. Put the remaining ingredients in a small saucepan and bring to the boil until all the ingredients are well combined and dissolved. Remove the saucepan from the heat and place the carrots in the mixture.

Allow to cool, then place in an airtight container for up to 1 week.

## Griddled shrimp & baby leek skewers with tamari lime glaze

Sweet, sour and sticky shrimp skewers, these make a tasty and easy appetizer.

12 prawns/shrimp, cleaned and deveined
4 baby leeks or spring onions/scallions, cut into 2.5 cm/1 in. pieces
50 ml/3½ tablespoons tamari
1 thumb-sized piece of ginger, grated
2 limes, 1 halved and 1 juiced
1 fennel bulb, sliced lengthways
2 tablespoons olive oil

*6 skewers*

SERVES 6

Place the prawns/shrimp, leeks or spring onions/scallions, tamari, ginger and the juice from 1 lime into a bowl and allow to marinate overnight (or for a minimum of 30 minutes).

Thread two prawns/shrimp and leeks or spring onions/scallions alternately on skewers. Heat the griddle and cook the prawns/shrimp for approx. 3 minutes on each side, basting with the tamari, ginger and lime glaze from the bowl. Arrange on a platter. Griddle the halved lime or serve fresh on the side of the platter.

Brush the fennel slices with the olive oil and griddle, turning once, until tender (approx. 2 minutes on each side). Add to the platter and serve.

# Baked salmon chops with vegetables

This is a simple dish that is easy to adapt for two people or to scale up (as long as you have enough oven space). The addition of the capers, pine nuts and currants at the end, along with the basil and parsley, enlivens this versatile all-in-one dish. It's a very generous feeling dish.

6 salmon chops (or fillets if you prefer)
1 lemon, thinly sliced
4 garlic cloves, thinly sliced
2 fresh bay leaves
2 tablespoons olive oil
500 g/1 lb. 2 oz. new potatoes, steamed
1 red onion, cleaned and thinly sliced
2 yellow or green courgettes/zucchini, sliced about 1 cm/ ½ in. thick
200 g/1 heaped cup vine-ripened cherry tomatoes
125 ml/½ cup dry white wine

40 g/⅓ cup pine nuts, toasted
40 g/⅓ cup currants, soaked in cold water for 10 minutes
2 tablespoons capers
sea salt and freshly ground black pepper
a handful of fresh basil, roughly chopped, to serve
a handful of fresh parsley, roughly chopped, to serve

*30 x 23 cm/12 x 9 in. (3 litre/6 pint capacity) baking dish*

SERVES 6

Place the salmon chops in a large bowl, season generously with sea salt and freshly ground black pepper, add the lemon, garlic, bay leaves and half the olive oil. Cover with clingfilm/plastic wrap and refrigerate until required.

Preheat the oven to 200°C (400°F) Gas 6.

Arrange the steamed potatoes, red onion, courgettes/zucchini and tomatoes in a single layer in the baking dish. Place the salmon on top of the mixture with the lemon and pour over remaining marinade, the wine and the remaining olive oil and bake in the preheated oven for 20 minutes. Remove from the oven and scatter with the pine nuts, currants and capers. Serve immediately, sprinkled with the fresh basil and parsley.

NB: if you use salmon fillets, the cooking time should be decreased by 5 minutes.

*Make it pretty*

Succulents are low in maintenance, but high in style. All they need is a little pot with some soil. When decorating a table, you can display them in votive candle holders, glass jars or little bowls.

# Pan-fried calamari with smoky chilli & lemon salt

This makes a great accompaniment to the shrimp skewers on page 99, and the flavoured salt is the perfect finishing touch.

**2–3 whole squid,**
**cleaned and scored,**
**tentacles reserved**
**1 tablespoon olive oil**
**½ teaspoon cracked**
**black pepper**

SMOKY CHILLI
& LEMON SALT
**1 dried and smoked**
**ancho chilli/chile**
**100 g/3½ oz. sea salt**
**grated zest and juice**
**of 1 lemon**

*baking sheet lined with*
*parchment paper*

SERVES 6 AS AN
APPETIZER OR MEZZE

Preheat the oven to 160°C (325°F) Gas 3.

First make the Smoky chilli and lemon salt. Blitz the ancho chilli/chile in a food processor into a fine dust. Add the sea salt and give it a few pulses. Add the lemon zest and juice and then spread the mixture on to the prepared baking sheet. Bake in the preheated oven for 20–25 minutes, making sure to keep breaking the mixture up with a fork. Remove from the oven and set aside. The salt will keep perfectly stored in an airtight container.

Preheat a frying pan/skillet over a high heat. Cut the squid into large pieces and combine with half the olive oil, the pepper and the reserved tentacles in a bowl. Fry in the frying pan/skillet, scored-side down, for 1–2 minutes until golden. Turn and cook the other side for 1–2 minutes until opaque and just cooked through. Transfer to a bowl and set aside. Serve topped with a pinch of the flavoured salt. Best eaten warm.

# Wakame, pear & daikon salad

This is a salad of contrasts – sweet and peppery and minerally saltiness. It's surprisingly refreshing.

**10 g/⅓ oz. dried**
**wakame seaweed**
**50 g/2 oz. daikon,**
**scrubbed and sliced**
**on a mandoline**
**50 g/2 oz. radish, thinly**
**sliced on a mandoline**
**2 pears (such as**
**Williams), shaved**
**on a mandoline**

MISO DRESSING
**1 tablespoon light soy**
**sauce**
**1 tablespoon rice wine**
**(mirin)**
**1 tablespoon cider**
**vinegar**
**juice of 1 lime**
**2 tablespoons shiro**
**miso**

SERVES 6

Place the wakame in a large bowl, cover with warm water and set aside to soak for 5 minutes, then drain well. If the wakame is in big pieces, chop it up into bitesize pieces (a similar size to the radish slices). Combine the radish and pears in a large bowl and add the drained wakame.

For the miso dressing, combine the soy sauce, rice wine, cider vinegar and lime juice in a bowl with 2 tablespoons water. Add the miso and whisk to combine.

Arrange the salad in a large serving bowl or on a plate, drizzle with the miso dressing and serve.

# Frozen yogurt cake

Allow this cake to sit for 10–20 minutes before serving, to make the texture slightly less 'crunchy'. The only way to avoid crystals forming would be to churn it, but as that is a faff, this way you have a super fresh and light frozen yogurt cake with fresh fruit.

### BASE
**70 g/5 tablespoons butter, melted**
**150 g/1½–2 cups ginger biscuits/ cookies, blitzed into crumbs**

### PEACH & YUZU LAYER
**2 x 400 g/14 oz. cans peaches in syrup, drained**
**80 ml/5 tablespoons coconut blossom syrup or honey**
**1 teaspoon vanilla paste**
**1½ tablespoons yuzu juice**
**500 g/2½ cups thick Greek-style yogurt**
**100 ml/⅓ cup double/heavy cream, lightly whipped**

### BLUEBERRY LAYER
**300 g/2¼ cups blueberries**
**100 g/scant ½ cup thick Greek-style yogurt**
**50 ml/3½ tablespoons coconut blossom syrup or maple syrup**
**peaches and blueberries, to serve**

*deep springform cake pan, 20 cm/ 8 in. round, greased and lined with parchment paper*

SERVES 6–8

To make the base, melt the butter in a large pan over a low heat. Stir the biscuit/cookie crumbs into the butter and mix until it looks like wet sand. Press the crumb mixture into the base of the cake pan in an even layer, then freeze.

In a blender or food processor, blitz the peaches with the honey, vanilla and yuzu until smooth, then add the yogurt and the lightly whipped cream. Pour the fruit mixture over the biscuit/cookie base and return to the freezer for up to 3 hours or overnight.

Meanwhile, rinse out the blender or food processor, and blitz the blueberries, yogurt and syrup. Add this layer to the cake pan and return it to the freezer.

The cake is ready as soon as the top layer is hard, but you can keep it in the freezer for as long as you like. Slice the cake while still frozen and serve with blueberries and peach slices.

# Pizza party

Nothing beats homemade pizza, so put down
the takeaway menus and have a crack at making
your own. This is such a great way to enjoy
this rustic yet contemporary sharing food.
Make them together for maximum enjoyment.

*Menu*

Whisky iced tea
Antipasti platter
Kale & pecorino pesto
Roasted mini aubergines
Cannellini bean salad
Roasted veg with pesto & leafy salad

*Pizzas* – Margherita
Green pizza
'Nduja, tomato & rocket
Squash, blue cheese & sage
Lamb & sumac pide
Feta & fig pide
Ricotta, blackberry & honey
Nutella, berries & ice cream

Marsala poached plums

## PARTY PLANNING

This is a super easy menu with only a little prep needed.

*The night before:*
- Start making the pizza dough the night before, let it stand at room temperature for 1 hour or until doubled in size, then place in the refrigerator. Alternatively, make it on the morning of your get-together.
- Make the poached plums and store in the refrigerator. Make the Almond & amaretto crunch and store.

*On the morning of the gathering:*
- Make the pesto, Roasted mini aubergines and Cannellini bean salad and set aside.
- Roast the veg for the salad and the butternut squash and set aside.
- Make the Lamb sumac pide filling, allow to cool and refrigerate.

*Two hours before your friends arrive:*
- Remove the dough from the refrigerator and allow it to come to room temperature.
- Start brewing the tea and chilling it.

*One hour before:*
- Set up the antipasti platter, bring the poached plums to room temperature.
- Turn the oven on. Place the pizza stone or an upside-down baking sheet in to preheat so it gets very hot.
- Finish the Whisky iced tea and scorch your peaches.

*When your friends arrive:*
- Serve them a Whisky iced tea and let them help themselves to the Antipasti.
- Knock back/punch down the dough, divide into 8 balls and allow them to rest under a clean kitchen towel.
- Let everyone help you make the pizzas and come up with new topping combos.
- Finish the salad and serve it with the pizzas.
- When you reach the sweet pizza stage, bring out the poached plums and Almond and amaretto crunch.

# Whisky iced tea

With the smokiness of the whisky, the tart sweetness of the peaches and aromatic vanilla, which enhances all the other flavours, this iced tea is a real winner.

**1 litre/4¼ cups water**
**6 peach-flavoured teabags**
**½ teaspoon vanilla extract**
**1–2 tablespoons agave, to taste**
**100 ml/⅓ cup peach nectar**
**150–200 ml/⅔–scant 1 cup whisky (depending how strong you like it)**

SCORCHED PEACHES
**3 peaches, stoned/pitted and quartered**
**1 tablespoon honey**
**1 teaspoon light brown sugar**
**a pinch of vanilla powder (optional)**

MAKES 6

Bring the water to the boil in a small saucepan. Remove the pan from the heat and add the teabags and vanilla and let steep for 5 minutes. Remove the teabags and stir in the agave until dissolved. Transfer to a jug/pitcher, add the peach nectar and stir to combine. Chill in the refrigerator for at least 1 hour.

Add the whisky to the jug/pitcher and pour into ice-filled glasses.

To scorch the peaches, place them on a baking sheet, drizzle with honey, top with sugar and grill/broil under a very hot grill/broiler until scorched. Serve in each glass, with extra on the side for people to nibble on. Top with a pinch of vanilla powder and serve.

# Antipasti platter

Antipasti literally means 'before the meal'. A combination of small bites of tasty food, usually accompanied by wine and meant to stimulate the appetite before digging into the main meal.

An antipasti plate will bring a relaxed spirit and friendly, casual conversation to your meal. No matter what the occasion, serving antipasti is the perfect way to slow things down and savour great food.

*A few tips:*
· Keep the antipasti simple so you don't crowd out the main meal.
· Antipasti should complement the meal you're planning no matter how modest or lavish. In the case of this menu it is very bread-based with all the different types of pizzas, so I have kept the bread that I am serving with the antipasti to a thin crispbread.
· It can be a combination of bought and home-made items, and always offer vegetarian options.

*Buy in:*
· Three types of cured meat
· Mozzarella balls with some lemon zest and olive oil
· Marinated artichokes
· Pickled peppers
· Black and green olives
· Fresh figs
· Marcona almonds or any type of roasted nut
· Pane carasau bread or another crispbread

*Recipes:*
· Kale & pecorino pesto
· Roasted mini aubergines
· Cannellini bean salad

## Kale & pecorino pesto

A twist on the classic with the addition of kale and pecorino. Good with a roasted vegetable salad and as part of a starter.

80 g/½ cup pine nuts
25 g/⅓ cup freshly chopped basil
25 g/⅓ cup flat-leaf parsley
50 g/1½ cups kale, stems removed
2 garlic cloves
60 g/1 cup grated Pecorino
140 ml/⅔ cup extra virgin olive oil
grated zest and juice of ½ lemon
sea salt and freshly ground black pepper

MAKES 1 JAR

Heat a small frying pan/skillet over a low heat. Add the pine nuts and cook until golden, shaking occasionally. Put into a food processor with the basil, flat-leaf parsley, kale, garlic, Pecorino and olive oil. Process until smooth, season and stir through the lemon zest and juice.

Any leftover pesto can be stored in a sterilized jar, topped with olive oil, in the refrigerator for up to a week.

## Roasted mini aubergines

A very simple addition to an antipasti platter.

350 g/6 or 7 mini aubergines/ eggplants, sliced in half
2 tablespoons olive oil
a handful of basil
sea salt and freshly ground black pepper

*baking sheet lined with parchment paper*

SERVES 6 AS AN APPETIZER

Preheat the oven to 180°C (350°F) Gas 4.

Place the aubergines/ eggplants on the prepared baking sheet, season with salt and pepper and drizzle with olive oil. Bake for 20 minutes in the preheated oven or until crisp and golden. Place into a bowl and top with basil.

## Cannellini bean salad

This salad is so adaptable – it can easily become a hearty salad with the addition of sautéed chorizo and rocket/ arugula. It's equally as nice in its simplicity with the sharp dressing and parsley.

400 g/14-oz. can cannellini beans
2 shallots, finely chopped
½ tablespoon sherry vinegar
juice of ½ lemon
4 tablespoons olive oil
a handful of flat-leaf parsley, roughly chopped
sea salt and freshly ground black pepper

SERVES 6 AS AN APPETIZER

Drain the beans and set aside. Place all the other ingredients in a serving bowl and whisk. Add the beans and serve.

*Maximize flavour*

Making the side dishes with some zing helps to balance the flavours. Lemon zest on the mozzarella balls and the citrus dressing on the beans cut through all the rich flavours.

# Pizza dough

A classic recipe, but one that you will come back to time and time again.

**6 g/1 teaspoon dried yeast**
**700 g/5 cups strong bread flour**
**2 pinches of sea salt**
**70 ml/scant ⅓ cup extra virgin olive oil**
**semolina, for dusting**

*pizza sheet or large baking sheet*
*pizza stone or large heavy baking sheet*

MAKES 8 PIZZAS

Combine the yeast and 100 ml/scant ½ cup lukewarm water in a bowl, stir to dissolve and set aside until foamy (approx. 5 minutes).

Combine the flour, salt and olive oil in an electric mixer fitted with a dough hook.

Add the yeast mixture and 320 ml/scant 1½ cups water and knead until well combined. Knead on a low speed in the mixer for approx. 5 minutes until a smooth, elastic dough is formed.

Let the dough stand at room temperature, covered with a damp kitchen towel, until doubled in size (1 hour) or refrigerate overnight to prove – this can be done the night before and brought to room temperature (approx. 2 hours) before you bake.

Turn out the dough onto a flour-dusted surface and knock back/punch down, then bring the mixture just together to form a smooth, soft dough. Do not overwork.

Divide the dough into 8 balls, then place on a lightly floured surface and cover with a lightly floured kitchen towel until doubled in size (20 minutes).

Working with one ball of dough at a time, place onto a semolina-dusted 22 cm/8½ in. pizza sheet and press outwards from the centre to flatten, making the edges slightly thicker than the centre (if you do not have a pizza sheet, use a baking sheet dusted with semolina).

Put a pizza stone or a large, heavy baking sheet upside down on the top shelf of the oven. Preheat the oven to 220°C (425°F) Gas 7 for at least 30 minutes.

Spread the base with pizza sauce, then transfer the base to the hot pizza stone or baking sheet. Add the toppings (see pages 113, 116 and 118), then bake in the preheated oven until the edges are puffed and golden and the base is crisp (12–18 minutes or according to the time specified in the recipe). Repeat with the remaining dough balls and serve hot.

## Margherita

3 tablespoons passata/
   strained tomatoes
1 mozzarella ball
a handful of basil
   leaves, plus extra
   to serve
1 teaspoon dried
   oregano
olive oil, to drizzle

sea salt and freshly
   ground black pepper

TO SERVE
chilli/chile oil

Prepare the dough and preheat the oven
(see Pizza dough recipe, page 112).

   Smooth the passata/strained tomatoes over
the bases with the back of a spoon. Scatter with
the mozzarella and herbs, drizzle with olive oil and
season. Bake for 8–10 minutes in the preheated
oven until crisp. Serve with a little more olive oil
or chilli/chile oil, and basil leaves.

## Green pizza

1 mozzarella ball, torn
75 g/1¼ cups tender-
   stem broccoli,
   blanched and cooled
1 small courgette/
   zucchini, thinly sliced,
   or 3 courgette/
   zucchini flowers and
   mini courgettes/
   zucchini

olive oil, to drizzle
3 tablespoons Kale
   & pecorino pesto
   (see page 110)
grated zest of 1 lemon
sea salt and freshly
   ground black pepper

Prepare the dough and preheat the oven
(see Pizza dough recipe, page 112).

   Scatter the dough with the mozzarella cheese,
broccoli and courgette/zucchini, then drizzle with
olive oil, season and add the Kale & pecorino
pesto. Bake for 8–10 minutes until crisp. Serve
with a little more olive oil and the lemon zest.

## 'Nduja, tomato & rocket

50 g/½ cup 'nduja
7 cherry tomatoes,
   halved
10 g/⅛ cup Parmesan,
   shaved
sea salt and freshly
   ground black pepper
olive oil, to drizzle

TO SERVE
a handful of basil leaves
a handful of rocket/
   arugula

Prepare the dough and preheat the oven
(see Pizza dough recipe, page 112).

   Spread the 'nduja over the base, scatter with
the tomatoes, Parmesan, salt and pepper and olive
oil. Bake for 8–10 minutes until crisp. Serve with a
little more olive oil, fresh basil and rocket/arugula.

## Squash, blue cheese & sage

100 g/3½ oz. butternut
   squash, sliced and
   roasted
60 g/½ cup blue
   cheese, crumbled
50 g/⅓ cup mozzarella,
   torn

approx. 10 sage leaves
   (depending on size)
olive oil, to drizzle
sea salt and freshly
   ground black pepper

Prepare the dough and preheat the oven
(see Pizza dough recipe, page 112).

   Scatter the dough with the butternut squash,
both cheeses and sage leaves, then drizzle with
olive oil and season. Bake for 8–10 minutes until
crisp. Serve with a little more olive oil.

# Lamb sumac pide

A Middle Eastern pizza topping including yogurt, pomegranate, fresh mint and lemon to enliven the senses.

2 tablespoons olive oil
1 brown onion, finely
    chopped
2 garlic cloves, crushed
1 teaspoon ground
    coriander
1 teaspoon sumac
¼ teaspoon ground
    cinnamon
¼ teaspoon chilli/hot
    red pepper flakes
2 fresh bay leaves
1 teaspoon dried
    oregano
½ teaspoon ground
    white pepper

250 g/9 oz. mince/
    ground lamb
2 tomatoes, roughly
    chopped
1 red (bell) pepper,
    diced
1 teaspoon
    pomegranate
    molasses

TO SERVE
olive oil, to drizzle
pomegranate seeds
fresh mint leaves
lemon wedges
yogurt

Heat 1 tablespoon of the olive oil in a large frying pan/skillet and fry the onion for 10 minutes until softened. Add the garlic and cook for a further minute, then add the coriander, sumac, cinnamon, chilli/hot red pepper flakes, bay leaves, dried oregano and white pepper. Cook for another 2 minutes, then add the lamb and fry for about 5 minutes until browned. Add the tomatoes and red (bell) pepper and cook gently for another 2 minutes, making sure that it stays moist. Stir through the pomegranate molasses and set aside until you are ready to use.

Use the Pizza dough recipe (see page 112) and gently knock back/punch down the dough to expel any large air bubbles. Sprinkle a little semolina onto a clean surface, then roll out the dough into a 30 x 20 cm/12 x 8 in. rectangle and quite thin. Spread the lamb mixture onto the dough, then fold the edges of the pizza over by 2 cm/¾ in. and pinch both ends to create a boat shape. Transfer the pide onto a baking sheet dusted with semolina. Bake in the oven for 10 minutes until the crust is cooked through and golden.

To finish, serve the pide with olive oil, pomegranate seeds, mint, a wedge of lemon and a dollop of yogurt.

# Fig & feta pide

As this cooks, the figs and honey caramelize to create a jammy consistency that pairs so well with the salty tanginess of feta cheese.

3 figs, sliced into
    rounds
100 g/¾ cup feta
    cheese, crumbled
2 tablespoons runny
    honey, plus extra
    to serve

olive oil, to drizzle
sea salt and freshly
    ground black pepper
fresh mint leaves,
    to serve

To make the pide, gently knock back/punch down the dough to expel any large air bubbles. Sprinkle a little semolina onto a clean surface, then roll out the dough into a 30 x 20 cm/12 x 8 in. rectangle and quite thin.

Spread the feta and figs onto the dough, then fold the edges of the pizza over by 2 cm/¾ in. and pinch both ends to create a boat shape. Drizzle over the honey, olive oil and season with salt and pepper. Transfer the pide onto a baking sheet dusted with semolina. Bake in the preheated oven for 10 minutes until the crust is cooked through and golden. Serve with an extra drizzle of honey and a few mint leaves.

# Roasted veg with pesto & leafy salad

I could eat this every day with many variations of roasted vegetables, but my all-time favourite combo is the roasted tomatoes with peppers. In my fridge there is always a batch of these tomatoes and they can really make a meal, whether it's breakfast, lunch, dinner or snack. On toast they are great with avocado, feta and rocket/arugula.

270 g/1½ cups cherry tomatoes on the vine
200 g/1½ cups mixed yellow and red romano peppers, roughly chopped
2 tablespoons olive oil
1 teaspoon honey
a pinch of chilli/hot red pepper flakes
sea salt and freshly ground pepper
a handful of rocket/arugula
1 tablespoon Kale & pecorino pesto (see page 110)

*baking sheet lined with parchment paper*

SERVES 6 AS A SIDE

Preheat the oven to 180°C (350°F) Gas 4.

Place the tomatoes and peppers on the prepared baking sheet. Drizzle with the olive oil, honey, chilli/hot red pepper flakes and salt and pepper. Bake in the preheated oven for 20 minutes until just cooked through, then allow to cool.

On a serving plate place the roasted vegetables and all their juices, top with the rocket/arugula and pesto.

## Ricotta, blackberry & honey

Is this a pizza or is it dessert? It does not matter because it is a great combination! The blackberries burst and ooze a little juice and mix in with the honey.

100 g/½ cup ricotta
½ teaspoon vanilla paste
100 g/1 cup blackberries
3 sprigs of lemon thyme, leaves picked, plus extra to serve

2 tablespoons honey, plus extra to serve
1 tablespoon slivered pistachios, to serve

Prepare the dough and preheat the oven (see Pizza dough recipe, page 112).

In a bowl mix the ricotta with the vanilla paste. Spread the ricotta over the base, scatter with the blackberries and lemon thyme leaves and drizzle with honey. Bake for 8–10 minutes until crisp. Serve with more honey, extra lemon thyme and the slivered pistachios.

## Nutella, berries & ice cream

Food heaven! This is inspired by a similar pizza that I had when I was last in Sydney. At the end of the meal we all shared the Nutella pizza with melting ice cream – a perfect end to the meal.

3 tablespoons Nutella
75 g/½ cup raspberries
3 strawberries, halved
1 large scoop vanilla ice cream

icing/confectioner's sugar, to serve

Prepare the dough and preheat the oven (see Pizza dough recipe, page 112).

Bake the plain base in the preheated oven for 6 minutes, remove and spread with the Nutella, then bake for another 2 minutes until crisp. Serve with the fresh berries, a scoop of ice cream in the centre and a dusting of icing/confectioner's sugar.

## Marsala poached plums

A simple, classic dish that can sit in the fridge and be brought out as a quick dessert. Perfect topped with the almond crunch.

700 g/1½ lb. plums
200 g/1 cup granulated/ caster sugar
300 ml/1¼ cups Marsala
3 star anise
1 vanilla pod/bean, seeds scraped

ALMOND & AMARETTI CRUNCH
100 g/1¼ cups flaked/ slivered almonds, toasted
50 g/2 oz. amaretti biscuits/cookies, crumbled

SERVES 6

Cut the plums in half and remove the stones/pits. Tip the sugar into a pan with the Marsala, star anise and vanilla seeds. Gently heat until the sugar dissolves. Slide the fruit into the syrup. Bring the pan to the boil, then let it simmer for 5–10 minutes, depending on the ripeness, until the plums are soft. Leave to cool slightly and store in the refrigerator for up to 1 week.

For the crunch, mix the almonds and crumbled biscuits/cookies together and store in an airtight container.

Celebrate the art of feasting, whether cooking
a sensual dinner for Valentine's Day or a special
event. This section is for making up those
platters or tables of food when you have more
time to spend in the kitchen.

# FEAST

# Celebration

This menu is all about grazing, sharing and feasting together.
On a platter or board place a selection of fruit and vegetables with
marinated feta, olives and flat breads for people to start grazing.
Then gradually bring out the dips, starting with the Sweet potato
and roasted garlic hummus, then Radish tzatziki and replenish the
flatbreads. Meanwhile, the lamb is gently cooking in the oven and
the Roasted beetroot and carrots are ready to be placed on the bed
of walnut skordalia. Add this to the selection for people to keep
grazing. Once the lamb is ready, allow it to rest, then bring to the
table with the cooking juices and the Quick fennel & dill pickle.
A feast of love.

## Menu

Rosé spritzer with rose tea buds

Sweet potato & roasted garlic hummus

Marinated feta

Roasted beetroot & carrots
with walnut skordalia

Radish tzatziki

Quick fennel & dill pickle

Lamb kleftiko

Roasted figs & grapes with
whipped ouzo yogurt

Almond crescents

## PARTY PLANNING

Get ahead and make it easy for yourself. First, remember that this is a feast – it will take a bit of extra work, but make sure it's done with love.

*A few days before:*
· Make the Almond crescents and store in an airtight container – be careful not to devour the lot before the get together!

*The night before:*
· Prepare the lamb – I find that (provided you have the space in the fridge) you can place all the ingredients in the baking dish and cover and it's ready to go in the morning. It takes a long time to cook but it's worth it.
· Make the skordalia and hummus (reserving some roasted sweet potatoes to garnish) and store in airtight containers and refrigerate. Alternatively, buy the hummus and top it with some cubed roasted sweet potatoes, a drizzle of olive oil and some toasted cumin seeds.

*In the morning:*
· Before you put the lamb in (approx. 5 hours before people are due to arrive), roast the fruit for the dessert and the vegetables for the Walnut skordalia and set aside.
· 4 hours before the start time place the Lamb kleftiko in the oven and allow to cook gently. Make the Quick fennel & dill pickle, Marinated feta, Radish tzatziki and Ouzo yogurt and set the table.

*When your guests arrive:*
· Serve them a drink, gently heat the vegetables for both the Walnut skordalia and Sweet potato & roasted garlic hummus and bring out the Marinated feta. Place all on the table with flatbreads and then bring out the lamb – share all the food.
· Finally, top the Ouzo yogurt with the fruit and bring along the Almond crescents and serve.

### Make it pretty

Freeze edible flowers by working in layers. Fill an ice tray half full with water, add flowers facing down, and freeze. Add more water to the top and freeze. Use the same method for citrus fruits. Have fun with these – cut them into rounds or wedges (a wedge is perfect for a G & T).

# Rosé spritzer with rose tea buds

Rose water has been used to add a distinctive flavour to drinks for centuries. A little goes a long way and, when combined with the rose tea buds, the subtle flavour and fragrance make this a magical drink.

**1 bottle light, crisp rosé (750ml/3 cups)**
**a large pinch edible dried rose petals or rose tea buds (approx. 18 buds)**
**a dash of rose water**
**500 ml/2 cups soda water**
**ice**

SERVES 6

Place a couple of ice cubes in each glass. Half-fill with rosé, top with 2–3 rose tea buds, a dash of rose water and top with a little soda water.

# Sweet potato & roasted garlic hummus

Hummus is always a crowd pleaser and this version has a sweet earthiness with the roasted garlic and sweet potatoes. If pushed for time, you could make the roasted sweet potatoes and swirl them through good-quality store-bought hummus.

1 large sweet potato, peeled and cut into cubes

2 garlic cloves, skin on and bruised

4 tablespoons olive oil

2 teaspoons cumin seeds

1 x 400 g/14 oz. can chickpeas/garbanzo beans, rinsed and drained

juice of 1–1½ lemons

2½ tablespoons tahini paste

sea salt and freshly ground black pepper

a pinch of chilli/hot red pepper flakes, to finish

a pinch of Dukkah (see page 98), to finish

SERVES 4–6 AS A SIDE

Preheat the oven to 160°C (325°F) Gas 3.

Place the sweet potato, garlic, 1 tablespoon of the olive oil and cumin seeds on a baking sheet and season with salt and pepper. Bake in the preheated oven for 40–50 minutes, then add the chickpeas/garbanzo beans and bake for a further 10–20 minutes. Remove from the oven, take out a handful of crisped sweet potatoes and chickpeas/garbanzo beans and set aside.

Whizz the rest of the sweet potato and chickpeas/garbanzo beans with the remaining olive oil, lemon juice, tahini and salt and pepper in a blender until smooth – loosen with a little water if you like. If you don't have a blender, mash with a fork or masher until smooth. Finish with the reserved sweet potato and chickpeas/garbanzo beans, the chilli/pepper flakes and dukkah.

## Maximize flavour

*Marinated feta* – not only does this look great, but this is a quick way to add some flavour to a simple cheese. It is perfect for a mezze table or to top a Greek salad. Marinate your feta by drizzling with 2 tablespoons extra virgin olive oil, 1 teaspoon cracked pink peppercorns, a pinch of fresh or dried oregano and some grated lemon zest.

# Roasted beetroot & carrots with walnut skordalia

This is a dish that is a great mezze, appetizer or side. It is so versatile as it's great eaten on its own with crumbled feta and a handful of rocket/arugula.

2–3 beetroot/beets
(approx. 500 g/18 oz.),
scrubbed and cut into
wedges
5 mixed purple and
orange carrots
(approx. 500 g/ 18 oz.),
scrubbed and cut in 3
2 tablespoons olive oil
sea salt and freshly
ground black pepper
6 sprigs of oregano or
1 teaspoon dried
oregano

SKORDALIA
1 potato, peeled and
cut into cubes
3 garlic cloves, peeled
100 g/¾ cup walnuts,
lightly toasted (some
reserved to garnish)
½ tablespoon red wine
vinegar
2 tablespoons olive oil
sea salt and freshly
ground black pepper

SERVES 4–6 AS SIDE

Preheat the oven to 180°C (350°F) Gas 4.

To make the skordalia, place the potato in a small saucepan of water and bring to the boil and cook until very soft. Drain, reserving some of the cooking water. Using a mortar and pestle crush the garlic with the walnuts until they are fully combined and become a creamy consistency. Add the garlic and walnut mixture and the vinegar to the potatoes. When they are thoroughly combined add the oil and mix by hand until you achieve the desired taste. Season with salt and pepper. Place in the fridge for at least 1 hour before you serve. You might find you need a little more vinegar or olive oil to get an appetizing texture and balance of flavours.

Place the beetroot/beets, carrots, olive oil, salt and pepper and oregano on a baking sheet and bake in the preheated oven for 50–65 minutes until cooked through and crispy around the edges. Remove from the oven and place heaped on a bed of skordalia, finished with a scattering of the reserved walnuts.

# Radish tzatziki

Slow-cooked meat, and lamb in particular, always goes well with tzatziki – the cool freshness of the cucumber and radishes and the richness of the meat are a classic marriage.

1 cucumber
a pinch of sea salt
500 g/2¼ cups Greek-style
  yogurt
1 garlic clove, crushed
juice of ½ lemon
5 radishes, thinly sliced (some
  reserved to garnish)
3 sprigs of mint, leaves picked
  and chopped, plus a little extra
  for garnishing
1 tablespoon olive oil
a handful of pomegranate seeds,
  to garnish (optional)

SERVES 4–6 AS A SIDE

Coarsely grate the cucumber (reserving some for garnish), sprinkle with a pinch of salt and squeeze out all the liquid. Tip into a bowl with the yogurt, garlic, lemon juice, radishes, chopped mint and olive oil and mix well. Finish with the reserved cucumber, radishes, mint and pomegranate seeds.

*Make it pretty*

Add simple greenery along the table and use your fresh fruit and vegetables to add vibrancy.

## Lamb kleftiko

This is my take on the traditional Greek dish. Its origins come from when freedom fighters, or kleftes (robbers), would prepare their lamb in clay ovens hidden in the Greek mountains with lots of lemon and dried oregano. My version of the dish has added vegetables, white wine and fresh oregano.

1 shoulder lamb, bone in (approx. 2 kg/ 4½ lb.)
1 leek, roughly chopped
2 red onions, peeled and cut into wedges
1 lemon, cut into wedges
3 tablespoons olive oil

6 sprigs of oregano or 1 tablespoon dried oregano
6 sprigs of rosemary
2 teaspoons sea salt
1 teaspoon pink peppercorns
200 ml/scant 1 cup white wine

SERVES 4–6

## Quick fennel & dill pickle

Complementing the lamb, this super easy and refreshing pickle provides vibrancy against the richness of the meat.

250 ml/1 cup white wine vinegar
200 ml/scant 1 cup water
3 tablespoons caster/ granulated sugar
1 teaspoon salt
1 small head of fennel, sliced finely

lengthways on a mandoline (fennel fronds reserved)
3 sprigs of dill (optional)
1 teaspoon peppercorns

*sterilized glass jar (see page 4)*

MAKES 1 JAR

Preheat the oven to 160°C (325°F) Gas 3.

Lay two long pieces of parchment paper on top of two long pieces of kitchen foil (they should be long enough to completely seal the lamb within) – one widthways and the other lengthways, to form a cross. Place the leek, red onions and lemon wedges in the centre of the parchment paper and toss with 1 tablespoon of the olive oil and some seasoning.

Bring up the sides of the foil and set the lamb on top of the vegetables. Top with the oregano, rosemary, salt, pink peppercorns, the remaining oil and the white wine and scrunch the foil together tightly to enclose the lamb completely. Lift into a roasting pan and roast in the preheated oven for 4½ hours until very tender.

Serve on a platter with the softened vegetables and the cooking juices on the side.

Put the vinegar, water, sugar and salt in a saucepan and bring to the boil. Remove from the heat and allow to cool.

Place the sliced fennel in a bowl. Once the liquor has cooled to room temperature, pour it over the fennel. Tip into a jar, add the dill and fennel fronds and peppercorns and keep in the fridge for up to one week. This is best made at least 1 hour before serving.

# Roasted figs & grapes with whipped ouzo yogurt

The ouzo yogurt adds a welcome counterbalance to the sweet jamminess of the fruit. That herbal anise flavour and the sourness of the yogurt offer a lovely comparison. The accompanying lightly orange-scented gluten-free almond biscuits can be made in advance. They have a crispy skin and a soft centre and just get better with age.

**6 figs, halved**
**200 g/1⅓ cups red grapes**
**2 tablespoons runny honey**
**250 g/9 oz. thick-set Greek yogurt**
**2 tablespoons ouzo**

*baking sheet, greased and lined with parchment paper*

SERVES 6

Preheat the oven to 180°C (350°F) Gas 4.

Place the figs and clusters of grapes on the prepared baking sheet and drizzle over 1 tablespoon of the honey. Bake in the preheated oven for up to 20 minutes. Allow to cool.

Put the yogurt, remaining honey and the ouzo in a bowl and whisk. Place the yogurt mixture on the base of a serving dish and top with the roasted fruit and juices. Serve with a bowl of the Almond crescents on the side.

# Almond crescents

**350 g/3½ cups ground almonds**
**230 g/scant 1¼ cups golden caster/granulated sugar**
**grated zest of 1 orange**
**3 egg whites, lightly beaten**
**1 teaspoon vanilla extract**
**100 g/1¼ cups flaked/slivered almonds**

*2 baking sheets, greased and lined with parchment paper*

MAKES 30

Preheat the oven to 180°C (350°F) Gas 4.

Combine the ground almonds, sugar and orange zest in a large bowl. Add the egg whites and vanilla extract and stir until the mixture forms a firm paste. Roll level tablespoons of the mixture in almond shapes. Roll into 9-cm/3½-in. logs, then shape to form crescents. Press the almonds onto the top. Place on the prepared baking sheets. Bake in the preheated oven for 15 minutes or until lightly browned. Cool on the baking sheets. Store in an airtight container for up to 2 weeks.

# Banquet Parisien

## Menu

Kir royale

Radishes, pinky salt & crusty
bread & butter platter

Green olive & tarragon tapenade

Salade de chèvre with
edible flowers

Estouffade de boeuf bourguignon

Black garlic & saffron butter

Vibrant bowl of greens

Mini leeks with vinaigrette

Luxurious mash

Individual chocolate or
grapefruit tarts

Nothing epitomizes dining elegance more than a meal in a Parisian bistro. This menu is a relaxed yet decorous way to have a special French feast at home. Say 'Bienvenue' to your guests with a classic Kir royale and a platter of radishes, crusty bread and tapenade, so make your next rendezvous or soirée extra-special with this Parisian-inspired meal.

# PARTY PLANNING

At first this menu may seem overwhelming, but I promise that if you plan and prep a little, it will all run smoothly.

*A day or two ahead:*
· Make the Estouffade de boeuf bourguignon and keep refrigerated – or make it a week or so in advance and freeze.

*The day before:*
· Make the Pinky salt and Green olive & tarragon tapenade and store.
· Make the pastry for the Individual chocolate or grapefruit tarts and blind bake the cases. Make the filling(s) but don't fill the tarts. Store the fillings in the fridge and the cases in an airtight container.

*In the morning:*
· On a platter place all the salad leaves for the Salade de chèvre with edible flowers and cover with clingfilm/plastic wrap and refrigerate.
· Make the dressing and set aside for later.
· Slice the baguettes and top with the goat's cheese and thyme, cover and set aside.
· Make the Luxurious mash and keep in a saucepan.

· Make the Mini leeks with vinaigrette – these will only get better as the day goes on.
· Finish off the tarts and set aside.

*One hour or so before your guests arrive:*
· Place the Estouffade de boeuf bourguignon in a saucepan on the stovetop ready to gently heat up.
· Make the Radishes, Pinky salt and Green olive & tarragon tapenade platter and place on the table.
· Place a large pot of water on the stovetop ready to cook the vegetables later.

*When your guests arrive:*
· Serve them a drink and toast the gathering!
· Let them help themselves to the radishes platter.
· Heat the water for the vegetables.
· Heat the grill/broiler and grill/broil the goat's cheese toasts. When ready, dress the salad and serve with the toasts.
· Gently heat the Estouffade de boeuf bourguignon. Place the vegetables in the water and cook. When ready, place on a plate, top with the butter, heat the mash and serve.
· All that's left is to serve the dessert.

## Pinky salt

This is actually a salt and pepper in one. The addition of dried edible flowers is reminiscent of Herbes de Provence, which can actually be substituted here if you can't find edible cornflowers or lavender.

**80 g/⅓ cup Himalayan pink coarse salt**
**5 g/1 teaspoon pink peppercorns**
**2 pinches of dried edible flowers (such as cornflowers, rose, lavender)**

Blitz the Himalayan salt with the peppercorns in a food processor into a fine salt, then stir through the dried flowers. Store in an airtight container.

## Kir royale

This French cocktail is the ultimate elegant cocktail and evokes thoughts of Paris and grand festivities.

**1 bottle Champagne (750ml/3 cups)**
**60 ml/4 tablespoons crème de cassis**
**6 blackberries**

SERVES 6

Pour 10 ml/2 barspoons of the crème de cassis into each glass and top with Champagne. Top each glass with a blackberry.

## Radishes, pinky salt, crusty bread & butter platter

The simplest of courses, but very French and very tasty!

**1 pot of Pinky salt (see page 136)**
**Green olive & tarragon tapenade (see right)**
**1 bunch of radishes**
**50 g/3½ tablespoons unsalted butter**
**1 sourdough baguette**

SERVES 6

Serve all the ingredients on a large platter for guests to help themselves.

## Green olive & tarragon tapenade

With the addition of tarragon, this is a twist on the classic.

**100 g/¾ cup green olives**
**1 tablespoon capers**
**a small handful of fresh parsley**
**1 garlic clove**
**3 tablespoons olive oil**
**3 sprigs of tarragon**
**freshly ground black pepper**

SERVES 6

Combine the olives, capers, parsley and garlic in food processor and finely chop. With the motor running, gradually add the oil and process until blended. Transfer the tapenade to bowl. Stir in the tarragon and season to taste with freshly ground black pepper.

## Salade de chèvre with edible flowers

What says Paris more than Salade de chèvre? I just love this salad and I like to add the radicchio as it adds a complexity and a slight bitterness. This pairs well with the walnuts and the creaminess of the goat's cheese. The addition of the edible flowers is for aesthetics – also inspired by the beauty of Paris.

120 g/¾ cup walnut halves, toasted
2 tablespoons sherry vinegar
60 ml/4 tablespoons walnut oil
2 teaspoons Dijon mustard
a drizzle of honey
240 g/1¾ cups goat's cheese
1 sourdough baguette, cut diagonally into 12 slices
12 sprigs of thyme
1 head butter lettuce
1 radicchio (pink, if in season)
1 small red gem lettuce
a punnet of edible flowers

SERVES 6

Preheat the oven to 180°C (350°F) Gas 4.

Spread the walnuts over a baking sheet. Bake in the preheated oven for 5 minutes or until lightly toasted. Set aside to cool.

Whisk the vinegar, oil, mustard and honey in a bowl and set aside.

Preheat the grill/broiler to medium-high. Cut the goat's cheese into 12 slices. Place the bread on a baking sheet and cook under the grill/broiler for 1 minute on each side or until light and golden. Turn and top each slice with a piece of goat's cheese. Spread the cheese to the edges of the toast and top with the thyme. Cook under the grill/broiler for 2 minutes or until the cheese softens.

Meanwhile, tear the salad leaves into a bowl and mix well. Lightly drizzle with half of the dressing and place onto 6 plates or a large platter. Top with goat's cheese toasts and walnuts, then drizzle over the rest of the dressing and top with edible flowers.

# Estouffade de boeuf bourguignon

Burgundy with mushrooms and bacon lardons – true comfort food. The gelatinous quality of beef shins cooked on the bone gives a new dimension to the dish, but by all means use a more traditional braising cut, such as braising steak, if you prefer.

2 tablespoons olive oil
6 pieces of beef shin (bone in), approx. 1.2 kg/2¾ lb.
175 g/6 oz. bacon lardons
1 onion, finely chopped
3 garlic cloves, finely chopped
1 tablespoon plain/all-purpose flour
2 tablespoons tomato paste
500 ml/2 cups red wine
500 ml/2 cups beef stock
1 tablespoon chopped fresh thyme
2 dried bay leaves
20 g/1½ tablespoons butter
300 g/10 oz. shallots or pearl onions, peeled
250 g/3¾ cups button mushrooms, halved
a handful of parsley, roughly chopped
sea salt and freshly ground black pepper

SERVES 6

Preheat the oven to 110°C (225°F) Gas ¼.

Heat 2 teaspoons of the oil in a flameproof casserole dish over a medium-high heat. Cook one-third of the beef for 2–3 minutes or until golden. Transfer to a plate. Repeat, in 2 more batches, with oil and remaining beef.

Heat the remaining oil in the dish. Add the bacon, onion and garlic. Cook, stirring occasionally, for 5 minutes or until golden. Add the flour and tomato paste. Cook, stirring, for 1 minute. Gradually add the wine, stirring constantly, until well combined. Add the beef, stock, thyme and bay leaves to the bacon mixture. Cover and bake in the preheated oven for 3 hours.

Meanwhile, melt the butter in a frying pan/skillet over a medium-high heat. Cook the shallots and mushrooms, stirring, for 5 minutes or until golden.

Add the mushroom mixture to the dish. Bake, covered, for a further hour. Stir in the parsley. Season with salt and pepper. Serve with mash (see page 143).

*Make it pretty*

To set the scene and create the atmosphere of a French bistro, light the candles, play some Edith Piaf and allow the food to take centre stage.

# Black garlic & saffron butter

Black garlic is a type of caramelized garlic. It is made by heating whole bulbs of garlic over the course of several weeks – a process that results in black cloves. The flavour is sweet and syrupy with a hint of balsamic vinegar. If you can't source black garlic, just use normal garlic with ½ teaspoon of balsamic vinegar instead.

100 g/1 stick minus
  1 tablespoon unsalted
  butter, at room
  temperature
2–3 black garlic cloves
  (or alternatively use
  normal), roughly
  chopped

a small pinch of saffron
  threads, in 1 teaspoon
  warm water
sea salt and freshly
  ground black pepper

SERVES 6

In a pestle and mortar, grind the butter with the garlic, salt and pepper and the saffron in the warm water. Store in the fridge.

# Vibrant bowl of greens

To make it easy, use the same large pot to cook the vegetables. By putting them in the pot at different stages, they will all be ready at the same time.

2 small Romanescos,
  halved, or 1 larger
  Romanesco cut into
  4 pieces
100 g/3½ oz. Chantenay
  carrots

200 g/7 oz. sugar snap
  peas
200 g/7 oz. green beans
100 g/3½ oz. asparagus

SERVES 6 AS A SIDE

Place the Romanesco in a large pot of salted boiling water and cook for 2 minutes. Add the carrots to the same pot and cook for another 2 minutes, add the sugar snaps and green beans and cook for 1 minute, then add the asparagus and cook for another minute. Drain and place onto a serving platter. Top with some Black garlic & saffron butter (see left).

# Mini leeks with vinaigrette

The addition of this light acidic dish served alongside the luxurious mash and the rich beef introduces a contrasting element that cuts through but also ties all the dishes together.

**12 small leeks, trimmed of tough green parts**
**3 tablespoons sherry vinegar**
**1 teaspoon Dijon mustard**
**6 tablespoons extra virgin olive oil**
**Pinky salt (see page 136), to serve**

SERVES 6 AS A SIDE

Add the leeks to a large pot of boiling water and cook for approx. 5 minutes over medium heat until soft but not mushy. Transfer the leeks to a large bowl of ice water to stop them from cooking further.

Whisk the vinegar, mustard and olive oil together in a small bowl. Arrange the leeks onto a serving platter, sprinkle with Pinky salt and drizzle with the vinaigrette.

These can be made a few hours earlier as the flowers develop as the day goes on.

*Maximize flavour*

A cross between a side and a pickle, the addition of the marinated leeks to this menu really helps cut through the richness of other dishes.

# Luxurious mash

Simple but made just a little more special with the addition of celeriac.

**900 g/2 lb. potatoes, peeled and cut into chunks**
**300 g/10½ oz. celeriac, peeled and cut into chinks**
**1 tablespoon wholegrain mustard**
**100 g/1 stick minus 1 tablespoon butter**
**4 tablespoons double/heavy cream**
**a pinch of chives, finely chopped**

SERVES 6 AS A SIDE

Bring a large pan of salted water to the boil, add the potatoes and celeriac and boil until soft. This should take approx. 20–25 minutes.

When the potatoes and celeriac are cooked, drain off the water and put back into the drained pan. Cover with a clean kitchen towel for about 4 minutes to absorb some of the steam, then add the mustard, butter and cream.

Whisk the mixture with a hand-held blender on slow and continue to break the mixture up, then gradually increase it to high and whip them up to a smooth creamy mash. Dot with the chopped chives before serving.

# Individual chocolate & grapefruit citrus tarts

When developing this recipe I couldn't decide if chocolate or grapefruit citrus would be best, so I kept both! The pastry makes 6 tarts, so double if making both fillings.

### PASTRY
**225 g/1¾ cups plain/all-purpose flour, plus extra for dusting**
**100 g/1 stick minus 1 tablespoon butter**
**a pinch of salt**
**1 tablespoon sugar**
**beaten egg, for glazing**

### CHOCOLATE FILLING
**150 g/1 cup finely chopped dark/ bittersweet chocolate**
**150 ml/2/3 cup double/heavy cream**
**2 egg, whisked**
**2 tablespoons maple syrup**
**1 teaspoon vanilla paste**

### GRAPEFRUIT FILLING
**grated zest and juice of 1 grapefruit**
**juice of 1 lemon**
**juice of 1 lime**
**150 g/¾ cup caster/granulated sugar**
**2 eggs, whisked**
**50 ml/3½ tablespoons double/heavy cream**

*6 tart pans (8 cm /3 in.), greased, parchment paper and baking beans*

SERVES 6

First make the pastry. Sift the flour into a large bowl, add the butter and rub in with your fingertips until the mixture resembles fine breadcrumbs. Stir in the salt and sugar, then add 2–3 tablespoons water and mix to a firm dough. Knead the dough briefly and gently on a floured surface. Wrap in clingfilm/plastic wrap and chill while preparing the filling.

To make the chocolate filling, place the chocolate and cream in a microwave-safe jug/ pitcher and heat for a minute on a medium heat. Take out and mix well – at this point keep an eye on it. It may need an extra 30 seconds to melt. Once melted allow to cool a little, then add the eggs, maple syrup and vanilla paste.

To make the grapefruit filling, pass the grapefruit zest and grapefruit, lemon and lime juice through a sieve/strainer into a jug/pitcher, add the sugar and stir well, then allow to sit for 10 minutes. Whisk in the eggs and cream.

Preheat the oven to 180°C (350°F) Gas 4.

Remove the pastry from the fridge. On a clean floured work surface, roll the pastry out and cut into 6 circles to fit the tart pans. Line each tart pan with the pastry and return to the fridge to chill.

Line the pastry tarts with parchment paper and fill with baking beans. Place the pans on a baking sheet and bake in the preheated oven for 15 minutes. Remove the baking beans and parchment paper. Bake for another 2–3 minutes, or until the pastry is dry and pale golden-brown. Set aside to cool in the pan then, using a sharp knife, cut away the overhanging edge.

Turn the oven temperature down to 110°C (225°F) Gas ¼.

Fill the tart pans with the chocolate filling or the grapefruit filling and bake for 20–25 minutes until set. Remove from the oven and allow to cool in the pans before serving.

# Springtime

The sun is starting to shine, the days are gradually getting longer and what better way to celebrate than a springtime lunch! This menu is a take on the traditional roast dinner with fresher touches. Spring has a bounty of amazing ingredients and it's time to celebrate them with much lighter dishes for brighter days.

## Menu

Elderflower sparkle

Spinach & ricotta dip
with flatbreads

Make-ahead primavera risotto

Courgette, carrot & horseradish
marinated salad with watercress

Parmesan-baked cauliflower

Smashed new potatoes

Roast rib of beef with shallot
& mustard sauce

Cheat's easy trifle Eton mess

# PARTY PLANNING

To stay unflustered and be the host with the most, here are just a few tips to help you get organized:

*On the morning:*
· Make the Spinach & ricotta dip and refrigerate.
· Prep the cauliflower and lay on a baking sheet with the seasonings; cover with clingfilm/plastic wrap.

*Two hours before your friends arrive:*
· Part-make the risotto and set aside.
· Turn the oven on and prep the beef.
· Make the trifle until the custard and refrigerate to set, and whip the cream and refrigerate.
· Place the beef in the oven, leaving a shelf free for the cauliflower, and make the shallot and mustard sauce and set aside.
· Boil the potatoes and smash them, place them on a baking sheet, ready to go.
· Prep the salad, make the dressing and set aside. Make sure you cover the salad.
· Set the table.

*Ten minutes before your friends arrive:*
· Place the cauliflower in the oven.

*When your friends arrive:*
· Make the drink – it's best when it's fresh – and serve it.
· Serve the dip with the flatbreads
· Remove the cauliflower from the oven when it's cooked and place the potatoes in.
· Finish the risotto and serve.
· Gently heat the sauce.
· Check the beef and when it's ready, clear the risotto plates, dress the salad and serve.
· Serve the beef, smashed potatoes, cauliflower and salad. If you are using the fresh horseradish, pass it around the table as an extra grating really enlivens the dish.

*To finish your meal:*
· Top the trifle with the whipped cream, meringues and fresh fruit.

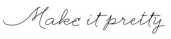

*Make it pretty*

A simple bowl of lemons on the table or used as a place setting adds a spark of colour to your spring vibe. If you can get the beautiful lemons with the leaves still attached, they make a lovely gift for your guests to take home.

## Spinach & ricotta dip with flatbreads

So quick to whip up and so full of flavour.

**a small handful of spinach, chopped**
**a small handful of rocket/ arugula, chopped**
**2 spring onions/scallions, finely chopped**
**½ garlic clove, crushed**
**250 g/1 cup ricotta**
**6 tablespoons yogurt**
**2 tablespoons olive oil**
**2 sprigs of parsley, roughly chopped**
**2 sprigs of dill, roughly chopped**
**2 tablespoons pesto**

**chilli/chili oil, to drizzle**
**sea salt and freshly ground black pepper**
**flatbreads, to serve**

SERVES 6

In a bowl mix the spinach, rocket/arugula, spring onions/ scallions, garlic, ricotta, yogurt, salt and pepper and olive oil. Swirl the herbs and pesto through and drizzle with chilli/ chili oil. Serve with flatbreads.

## Elderflower sparkle

Add some sparkle to your Spring day with this light refreshing drink. Adding the gold leaf brings a touch of bling to your day.

**20 ml/4 teaspoons elderflower liqueur**
**120 ml/½ cup vodka**
**1 lemon, sliced**
**soda water**
**ice**
**gold leaf (optional)**

MAKES 6 SMALL GLASSES

Fill a jug/pitcher with ice and pour in the liqueur, vodka, sliced lemon and soda water. Top each glass with gold leaf and serve.

# Make-ahead primavera risotto

Another fresh and light dish that would stand up well served on its own.
If you decide to make this ahead of time, it's best only to par-cook it.
If you try to make risotto ahead completely and then reheat it, it will be
overcooked and mushy. Instead, you can cook it until it is about halfway
done (the rice should still be rather firm inside) and then spread it out
on a baking sheet to stop cooking and cool. Finish the cooking process
just before you serve.

1.3 litres/5½ cups vegetable
  stock
200 g/7 oz. mixed green
  vegetables (such as asparagus,
  green beans, broccoli and
  sugar snap peas) and mini
  carrots, cut into bitesize pieces
1 leek, thinly sliced
1 tablespoon olive oil
1 tablespoon butter
1 celery stick, finely chopped
3 garlic cloves, crushed
350 g/1¾ cups arborio rice
100 ml/⅓ cup white wine
100 g/1½ cups grated Parmesan
3 sprigs of lemon thyme, leaves
  picked
a handful of parsley, roughly
  chopped
a pinch of chives, roughly
  chopped
a pinch of freshly grated nutmeg
a handful of fresh basil leaves
sea salt and freshly ground
  black pepper

SERVES 6 AS A STARTER

Place the stock and 250 ml/1 cup cold water in a large saucepan
over a high heat. Cover and bring to the boil. Add the carrots and
reduce the heat to medium. Simmer, covered, for 2 minutes. Add
the mixed green vegetables. Simmer, covered, for 2 minutes or until
just tender. Transfer the vegetables to a bowl with a slotted spoon.
Cover to keep warm. Remove the stock from the heat and, if making
in advance, set aside 100ml/⅓ cup (this will be used for reheating).

Add the leeks, oil and butter to a separate heavy-based pan and
cook for 3 minutes, then add the celery and garlic and cook on a low
heat for 5 minutes or until softened. Add the rice. Cook, stirring, for
1 minute. Add the wine. Simmer for 30 seconds. Add 100 ml/⅓ cup
stock to the rice mixture. Cook, stirring, until the stock has been
absorbed. Repeat with remaining stock, 100 ml/⅓ cup at a time,
until all the liquid has been absorbed and the rice is tender.

If making the risotto in advance, remove the risotto from the
stove and pour onto a baking sheet to stop the cooking and cool
as quickly as possible. (The rice will taste a bit raw in the centre.)
Refrigerate, uncovered until cold. The risotto can then be stored
in a covered container for up to 2 days. Note: eliminate this stage
if you don't want to make it in advance, and continue as below.

To reheat and finish cooking, return the risotto to the pan with
the reserved 100ml/⅓ cup stock. Heat gently until the liquid has
absorbed and the rice is tender. Add the vegetables, thyme, parsley,
chives, a grating of nutmeg and 50g/¾ cup Parmesan to the pan.
Stir. Remove from the heat. Stand, covered, for 2 minutes or until
the vegetables are heated through and the cheese has melted.
Season with salt and pepper. Stir in the basil and serve, topped
with the remaining Parmesan.

# Courgette, carrot & horseradish marinated salad with watercress

A light, punchy side salad to accompany the meat and potatoes.

200 g/1½ cups mini courgettes/zucchini, thinly sliced lengthways
200 g/7 oz. chantenay carrots, thinly sliced lengthways
juice of ½ lemon
3 tablespoons olive oil
100 g/1 cup watercress
½ teaspoon fresh horseradish, grated or 1 teaspoon cream horseradish
sea salt and freshly ground black pepper

SERVES 6 AS A SIDE

In the serving dish mix the courgettes/zucchini and carrots and dress with the lemon juice, olive oil and salt and pepper. Allow to sit for 30 minutes, then top with the watercress. Toss after you take to the table, then grate with horseradish.

# Parmesan-baked cauliflower

This versatile, easy and delicious dish has become my standby feed-a-crowd dish or mid-week meal. Also great finished with rocket/arugula and crispy bacon.

2 cauliflowers, sliced
    vertically into 5 cm/
    2 in. steaks
2 banana shallots,
    quartered
6 sprigs of lemon
    thyme, leaves picked
3 garlic cloves

3 tablespoons olive oil
20 g/¼ cup grated
    Parmesan
sea salt and freshly
    ground black pepper

SERVES 6 AS A SIDE

Preheat the oven to 180°C (350°F) Gas 4.
    Place the cauliflower steaks on a large rimmed baking sheet with the shallots, thyme leaves, garlic and olive oil; season with salt and pepper. Roast in the preheated oven for 30–35 minutes until almost tender. Sprinkle with Parmesan, and continue to roast for 10–12 minutes until the cauliflower is tender.

# Smashed new potatoes

An easy way of making potatoes as a side. Leaving the skin on helps to crisp up the edges when baked in the oven.

750 g/26 oz. mini new
    potatoes or Jersey
    Royals
40 g/3 tablespoons
    butter
sea salt and freshly
    ground black pepper

a large handful of
    chives, roughly
    chopped
a small handful of
    parsley, roughly
    chopped

SERVES 6 AS A SIDE

Place the potatoes in a pan of boiling water and cook until tender, approx. 18 minutes. Remove, drain and place on a baking sheet. When the potatoes have cooled a little, smash them with your palm to break them up a bit. Let them sit until 15 minutes before you need to serve them.
    While the beef is resting (see page 154), pop the potatoes, with the butter and salt and pepper, in the oven (which will be at 140°C (275°F) Gas 3 from cooking the beef) for 15–20 minutes, then top with the herbs and serve.

# Roast rib of beef with shallot & mustard sauce

This is a show stopper – nothing is more impressive than walking to a table carrying a rib of beef. The perfect way to celebrate the start of Spring!

2.5 kg/5½ lb. rib of beef
2 tablespoons olive oil
sea salt and freshly ground
    black pepper

SHALLOT & MUSTARD SAUCE
2 tablespoons butter
200 g/2 cups banana shallots,
    peeled and halved lengthways
2 garlic cloves, crushed
200 ml/scant 1 cup white wine
200 ml/scant 1 cup good-quality
    beef stock (stock cube is fine)
1 teaspoon lemon thyme leaves
1 teaspoon wholegrain mustard
a pinch of sugar, if desired
1 tablespoon chopped tarragon
    or parsley

SERVES 6

Preheat the oven to 220°C (425°F) Gas 7.

Place the joint of beef in a roasting pan, season with sea salt and freshly ground black pepper and drizzle over the olive oil.

Roast in the preheated oven for 20 minutes, then turn the oven down to 140°C (275°F) Gas 3. Cook for 20 minutes per 450 g/1 lb. for medium/15 minutes per 450 g/1 lb. for rare.

Rest the meat for 15–30 minutes in a warm place.

Meanwhile, to make the sauce, in a sauté pan melt the butter over a medium heat and place the shallots cut-side down to caramelize and brown – this should take 10–15 minutes. Then flip them over and cook for a further 5 minutes. Remove most of the shallots, leaving 3 in the pan and add the crushed garlic and the white wine. Turn up the heat and allow the wine to cook down by half. Add the stock and allow to simmer for 5 minutes. Add the beef cooking juices once rested, along with the lemon thyme and mustard and cook for another 5 minutes. At this point add the reserved shallots back in and turn the heat down. Taste and if it's too acidic, add a pinch of sugar. Take off the heat and add the tarragon or parsley. Serve alongside the beef.

Cut the meat away from in between the bones or separate the bones and serve as they are.

*Maximize flavour*

If you can source fresh horseradish, it makes a great pairing with beef. It is a member of the mustard family and releases a distinctive aroma when bruised or cut and has a very hot, peppery flavour that is more powerful than mustard. Pass it around the table, letting your guests freshly grate it onto their own plate. Grate what you need and if you have some left over, freeze it in smaller quantities.

## Cheat's easy trifle
## Eton mess

Have fun with this recipe and add your
own touches – if I don't have any meringues,
I like to add the flaked almond and amaretti
mixture from page 118 for crunch. Or in
high summer I make a tropical version,
with fruits such as mangoes and
passionfruit and coconut rum.

500 g/18 oz. good-quality
shop-bought custard
1 teaspoon cornflour/cornstarch
(optional)
a small Madeira loaf cake (approx
450 g/1 lb.), cut into cubes
110 ml/scant ½ cup berry liqueur
such as Chambord (reserving
1 tablespoon for the whipped
cream)
100 g/3½ oz. ready-made
meringues, broken
400 ml/1½ cups double/heavy
cream
1 teaspoon vanilla extract
1 tablespoon icing/confectioner's
sugar
seasonal berries, to finish

BERRY SAUCE
500 g/2½ cups frozen mixed
berries
2 tablespoons golden caster/
granulated sugar
1 teaspoon vanilla paste

SERVES 6

To make the berry sauce, place the frozen
berries into a saucepan with the sugar and
vanilla paste and cook on a medium heat until
juicy but the berries still have body. Allow to
cool and refrigerate until you're ready to serve.

To make the trifle, if you prefer a thicker
set custard gently heat the store-bought custard
in a saucepan with a teaspoon of cornflour/
cornstarch until thickened. Cover with a piece
of clingfilm/plastic wrap directly on the custard
to prevent a skin from forming. Alternatively,
use the custard straight from the container.

Layer the cake pieces in a glass presentation
bowl and drizzle with the berry liqueur (reserving
1 tablespoon for the cream). Spoon over the berry
sauce, add a layer of meringue and top with the
custard. Chill until the custard has set.

Whip the cream with the vanilla extract,
icing/confectioner's sugar and reserved berry
liqueur until just holding its shape. Spoon the
whipped cream on top of the custard, arranging
the remaining meringue pieces around it.
Decorate with seasonal berries and chill until
ready to serve.

# Index

## Acknowledgements

*Thank you for your generous contributions:*

Alison Satasi, owner of Luma in Barnes, London, for lending us your gorgeous props.

Azar Afshari, owner of Blue Lavender in Barnes, London, for your breathtaking flowers.

Catherine LeBlanc, for your craft beer expertise and fabulous cheese and beer pairing notes.

Sarah Fassnidge and India Whiley-Morton, for testing and tasting recipes – your contributions are invaluable. And also to Sarah for your assistance in more ways than one during the shooting of this book – you are and will be a superstar!

Mowie Kay – thank you for your stunning photographs and beautiful manner, just a pleasure to be around.

Jennifer Kay – the props just brought the food to life and I am forever grateful.

*At Ryland Peters & Small:*

Megan Smith – thank you for your guidance, expertise and infectious laughter! It did not feel like work as it was so much fun.

Editors Miriam Catley and Gillian Haslam, for your patience and tireless editing.

Art Director Leslie Harrington and Editorial Director Julia Charles, for kind words and creative leadership.

Publisher Cindy Richards, for the opportunity to bring this idea to life.

And to friends and family around the globe – thank you is not enough as this book is for and about you.

Finally, the biggest thank you goes to Matthew.